Writing Within Walls

Edited by
Arkbound Foundation

Arkbound
Building futures, Bridging divides

Writing Within Walls
Edited by the Arkbound Foundation

© Arkbound Foundation

ISBN: 9781912092161

First published in 2021
by Arkbound Foundation (Publishers)

Cover image by Hannah K. Lee

Arkbound is a social enterprise that aims to promote social inclusion, community development and artistic talent. It sponsors publications by disadvantaged authors and covers issues that engage wider social concerns. Arkbound fully embraces sustainability and environmental protection. It endeavours to use material that is renewable, recyclable or sourced from sustainable forest.

Arkbound
Backfields House
Upper York Street
Bristol, BS1 8QJ

www.arkbound.com

Writing Within Walls

Acknowledgments

This book represents the culmination of work across 14 months – from individual mentoring to the launch of a national competition. We are grateful to all of those who helped make it possible: the mentors and mentees, the writers themselves, together with support from organisations who helped raise awareness of the national competition. In particular, we would like to thank David Kendall; Stephen Luke from Jailmail; Geof, Nicki and Lubia from the Prisoners Advice Service; Victoria Sadler and her team at Clinks, as well as our fantastic three judges who had to work under a tight deadline for the national competition.

Laura Wood, who put in so much time as a volunteer and coordinator, deserves a huge shout out, together with all the volunteers we worked with, going right back to the beginning of 2020. Also Tasmin Briers, for her great design work and ideas.

For their on-going encouragement and passion for rehabilitation, we would additionally like to thank Rosemary and Ian at HMP Standford Hill, Kimberley from HMP Pentonville, together with Lady Val from the Corbett Network and our own Val, who puts in so much time as a trustee.

Last but not least, we are grateful to the individuals and funds who donated to make this book possible as part of the Writing Within Walls project. For a small charity that receives very little other funding, their support has made a huge difference.

OLD POSSUM'S
PRACTICAL TRUST

Editorial note

For safeguarding, we have used the initials or a given nickname for each contributor.

In some cases, to make a piece unique, we have changed its title. Apart from standard editing and proofreading (light), no other changes have been made to the content.

Contents

Foreword

By Eoin Mclennan-Murray

The UK prison population in 2020 stood at 78,700 - an increase of 18% from 2000 and the highest in Western European countries. The vast majority of people are incarcerated for financially orientated offences, with the average age range being 30-39. Studies by the Prison Reform Trust and Howard League have revealed that around 72% of prisoners suffer from one or more mental health difficulties, ranging from depression to ADHD.

Behind these statistics are stories of broken lives, of people who made the wrong turning in life, perhaps as a result of circumstances beyond their control. Where we may be swift to condemn some cases as a result of greed, recklessness or cruelty, the fact remains that the vast majority of serving prisoners come from disadvantaged backgrounds. Nearly all of them are due to re-enter society, and the success of their reintegration in many ways depends upon their experience of custody. Unfortunately, at the time of writing, the UK prison estate is going through what can only be described as another crisis.

The national Covid-19 pandemic has struck a devastating blow to all prisons. This comes hot on the heels of the irreparable harm done following Grayling's cost cutting of prison/probation budgets that left both services devastated. Their partial recovery was slow and has now been stopped dead in its tracks by Covid-19. Prison regimes have been sacrificed, 23 hour bang up is the norm and the essential lifeline of social visits abandoned. It is hardly surprising that with this backdrop levels of self-harm rocket to record highs.

What we can do, however, is seek to provide a beacon of light and opportunity to those who would otherwise languish in darkness. Trapped in their cells, few things are able to reach prisoners – but writing is one of them. It has the power to encourage and develop creative talent, as well as building confidence, self-esteem and later employment prospects. Moreover, it provides a means for prisoners to convey their perspectives and experiences, thus shedding light on things that we may otherwise misjudge or be unaware of.

These stories have all been written by people in prison. They represent the winning entries of a national writing competition that Arkbound Foundation ran in 2020. All pieces touch upon that most ephemeral yet enduring aspect of human character: hope. The reader cannot help but be moved by some of these stories and it is remarkable that in such times of penal adversity there are those who are able to lift people up and sustain them when all else seems defeated. For many, it is hope that has kept them alive.

When reading through this book, I hope you can pause for a moment to think about the many people in prison and cast aside prior prejudice and judgement.

- *Eoin Mclennan-Murray, February 2021.*

* * *

Eoin was former President of the Prison Governors Association, having worked in Her Majesty's Prison Service since 1978, including as a Governor for 20 years. Upon retirement in 2015, he has acted as Chair of trustees for the Howard League for Penal Reform and an advisor to the Justice Select Committee, as well as a patron of the Arkbound Foundation.

All that Remained in Pandora's Box

By Ophrys

John and I were fifteen when we went in search of the truth. We read Kafka, T.S. Elliot and Dostoevsky and we joined the local druids who met on the downs around dusk. The first time we attended, cycling there, the chief druid pointed out that we were on a major ley line – a site of power.

One Saturday afternoon, walking on my own along this same ley line which passed two miles north of where I lived, I searched for enlightenment – but it wasn't about. Instead, being interested in natural history, I saw a kestrel, a roe buck, a lesser spotted woodpecker and grove of dark green broom stunningly festooned in small flowers. The southerly breeze blew through the nearby birches, which shimmered with the light falling on their leaves and soughed like a chant - half whispered and half sung.

The druid had told me that nearby stood another ley line intersection and there was a place of ancient power. When he told me this, I could smell tobacco smoke – old Holbourn, I think – on his breath. I found the place. Dark elders grew there, around a rabbit warren. Above me swifts soared in circles, their sickle-shaped silhouettes like strange symbolic ciphers, high up in the sky. They seemed to convey a truth I couldn't quite read or understand.

John and I attended a Catholic grammar school. It had a good reputation for academic excellence and also for providing a traditional religious background which the governors, headmaster and staff felt gave us all we needed – but it did not. There was something else, we were sure; something more, but how did we access it? There was a kind of unfulfilled spiritual or philosophic hunger in us: a need to understand the meaning of life. John, more secular than myself, investigated Communism and Marx while I was drawn to Eastern mysticism and read Hermann Hesse – or tried to. Catholicism required faith but I had doubt. I liked the quotation:-

"Believe those who seek the truth, doubt those that find it."

After reading about astral travelling and Eric Van Danniken (who maintained "God was an astronaut"), John and I joined the southern UFO investigation society. They met regularly on clear nights, in the same down area frequented by the druids.

"Mumbo Jumbo!" The chief UFOlogist said, when I mentioned them. "They are as bad as the religious! Science is where the answers are, and the truth is undoubtedly out there." He pointed to the sky. The same place as heaven, I thought.

"The UFO pilots travel definite routes," said the UFOlogist. "This place is above a major magnetic point like at Warminster Down or Stonehenge - all navigation loci." The druids said something similar, I thought. Behind the man talking at me, two hares leaped over the turf, over the vetches, thyme and milkwort, quaking grass and fescues. From a spinney over the scarp slope, a tawny owl called.

The druids, the UFO hunters and the Catholics all had faith. Even Atheists did. I wondered about this as the dusk slid into darkness and the Plough began to appear. When it did, I searched for the Pole Star. As the darkness intensified, the lovely Pleiades appeared – the seven daughters of Atlas and Pleione forever transformed into stars. I doubted many things, but beauty stood alone – unequivocal; personal, maybe, but to me as real as hunger.

Some of the UFOlogists, like the druids, brought alcohol and a few smoked what John said was hashish. Both the UFO searchers and the pagans became equally stupid as they became inebriated or stoned. No alien craft appeared that night, nor the couple of other times I went along. I rather wondered if any potential aliens visiting here might be like older versions of John and I, in search of the truth. I looked at the laughing fools swigging from their bottles and hoped the aliens would keep away – fly on by.

John told me that political and economic perspectives were the only valuable viewpoints for understanding society and therefore ourselves. He said Marx was the basis of this understanding and more relevant than Jesus Christ or the Buddha. I didn't argue. I was vaguely interested but nothing like he was. He proposed a visit to Marx's tomb in Highgate cemetery, north London. I thought it rather a good idea: the cemetery was reputed to be good for wildlife. I suggested we go to the Marque Club in Soho. There were always a few good blues bands playing and we could get the last train back.

On the way up, John read The Communist Manifesto while I read Verse and Worse, an anthology of comic and curious verse. At one point, near Satwick, John started on about the class war and the materialist concept of history. I wondered if he still liked Thomas Hardy or H.G. Wells or the Beano - or was he an irrevocably committed Communist? I mentioned his obsession to my father, who told me that his brother - my uncle – had become an ardent Communist when he was John's age. He had then got into journalism, writing about class wars and so forth, only to become successful and buying a house in Muswell Hill, where he lived thereafter. What my friend would call a Bourgeois lifestyle. John seemed to ignore my own rather Bourgeois background, especially when he came to lunch or tea and accepted second – sometimes third – helpings from my mother who, he said, was a much better cook than his own. Communism vanished when my father offered him yet another Lyon's chocolate cupcake or a Mr Kipling almond slice.

"John talks the Left and eats the Right", my father said quietly to me.

Outside the train window, Oxford Ragwort grew out of the sleepers carrying the rails and flashed golden yellow. The train wheels rattled in triplets: trumpty-trump, trumpty-trump, trumpty-trump; 1,2,3; 1,2,3;1,2,3; Faith, Hope, Charity; Faith, Hope, Charity. That was the rhythm!

At the weekly assembly taken by Father Wake, faith, hope and charity were common topics he chose to speak on. Faith was important – no, it was vital - but somehow, I lacked it. Charity? Well, I had enough money on me to treat John to the Marquee or a kebab later if he was hard up... but Hope, that was really strong in me. Hope welled in my heart all the time. It was, I recalled, all that was left in Pandora's box when she opened it and all the evils flew out into the world.

I hoped they'd stop cutting down the Amazon Rainforest. I hoped they would not build on the old pastures opposite my home where, each Autumn, rings of horse mushrooms appeared, and my mother and I picked them. I hoped I would be a Zoologist and natural history author. I hoped people would be less greedy. I hoped John would, before long, talk less about Marx and Engles and we could once more talk about books, read Proust or Joyce and discuss it all. I hoped, when we got to Highgate, amongst the old headstones, I'd see some good butterflies or hear blackcaps singing, maybe even a nightingale. I hoped John would be happy with his visit.

They say "Hope springs eternal in the human breast" and I have to say, fifty years on from John, Karl Marx and myself that remains true to this day as I sit, looking through my cell window at the tree where there perches a robin, singing his winter song and it's so lovely and yet, so sad.

Swimming Against the Tide

By Mark A

"Precisely because the lager was a great machine to reduce us to the beasts, we must not become beasts; that even in this place one can survive, and therefore one must want to survive, to tell the story, to bear witness" – Primo Levi.[1]

A powerful, deeply instinctive force has driven human endeavour and spurred on remarkable feats of endurance throughout history. From gulags to torture chambers, mountain tops to ocean waves, epic stories emerge of survival against the odds that inspire and amaze us all. It is Hope, a distant light that flickers in the darkness of despair, capturing the corner of your eye. The source is unclear, but the warmth it offers is irresistible. Hope, for a future tomorrow that won't be like today, beckons us forward. You may feel alone in this moment, but you are not the first to walk this path. The way is lit by our forefathers, heroes and icons, sung and unsung. As Terry Waite reflected, chained to a radiator in Beirut, *"I have now entered a new fellowship, a unique fellowship of endurance... I need the support of others who have suffered... become one with them. Hold on to the light and hope, hope, hope."* [2]

---

1   Primo Levi, *'If this is a Man'*, (1958)
2   Terry Waite, *'Taken on Trust'*, (London, Hodder and Stoughton, 1994) pp.23, 105

Staring at the tired walls of my own prison cell, as one day melts inexorably into the next, I often find myself taking comfort in these extraordinary examples of untold hardship. *'If they could make it through that, what excuse do I have?'* And yet, just how does one adjust to the prospect of spending so many years of one's life in captivity, removed from the world and isolated from those we love? Condemned to watch but never participate, to yearn but never fulfil, to reach out but face rejection.

The bleak conclusion of academics that prisoners – struggling to find meaning and purpose, overcome by shame and remorse, and daunted by the misty abyss of time – simply learn to *"swim with the tide"* might sound rather unsurprising in the context of all this misery.[3] *"A life sentence kills your hope man, it takes it... it swallows it."*[4]

In a recent study in England and Wales about the ways in which people adapt to long-term imprisonment, researchers concluded that, for most long-term prisoners, their initial instinct is to respond reactively, defensively and often negatively to the crisis – looking backwards at what has been lost, rooted to the past. [5] Over time, however, this gives way to a new form of *'productive'* agency in which prisoners become more 'future-orientated'. As one female lifer put it, *"something switches in you where you find this inner*

---

3   Ben Crewe, Susie Hulley, Serena Wright (2007), 'Swimming with the Tide, Adapting to long-term imprisonment', *Justice Quarterly*, 34 (3), pp. 517-541; pp. 519, 537
4   Ben Crewe, 'Coping and adaptation', chapter 5 in – *'Life imprisonment from young adulthood'*, (London, Palgrave Studies in Prisons and Penology, 2020), pp. 125-207, p.164
5   Ibid., p.126

strength that you never knew you had." [6]

The problem is that *'productive'* here is interpreted as *'passive'* and conformist, *"yielding to rather than opposing the flow of life."*[7] Whilst this may be true for some, might there not be another side that previous scholars have missed? The story of human resilience, of Hope, would seem to suggest a very different view of survival in captivity. After all, *'Hope'* engenders a refusal to accept the nature of one's present condition as somehow inevitable, final or irredeemable. If the binary response to imprisonment is to *'sink or swim'*[8], that need not mean that everyone breaks out into front crawl.

Seen in this way, Hope is an act of resistance, not surrender or acceptance of one's fate. The desire to change one's circumstances in the wake of catastrophe means believing that change is both necessary and possible.

Of course, there are certainly moments in prison when the precariousness of our existence becomes all too painfully clear. There will be those amongst us for whom that distant flame of Hope has been altogether extinguished - and without Hope, there can be no life. The eyes deadened, faces sullen of the man or woman who gave up long ago haunt every jail. *"I think something's died inside me. Hope."* [9]

Last year alone claimed the lives of more than 300 prisoners in England and Wales, a rate 6 times higher than the general

---

6   Crewe et al. (2017), Ibid. pp.521, 524
7   Ibid., p.537
8   Ibid., p.524
9   Crewe et al. (2020), Ibid, p.201

population.[10] Seeing our own pain mirrored in their own, compassion – for a moment – gives way to fear. Others, desperate to numb the loss of former lives, turn to substance abuse or self-harm, with each ignominious year heralding its perverse new record-high statistic in a sea of self-destruction.

So there is undoubtedly some truth in the idea that a lot of prisoners eventually come to *"accept that they cannot escape the water or the direction of its flow"*[11], but it is a truth perhaps best expressed through the 'serenity prayer.' Having the wisdom to know the difference between what one can control and what one cannot is fundamental to happiness in all forms of life, inside or outside of the prison. As one prisoner describes, *"All you've got is hope. That's all I've got, and it's like no matter what plans you make, you're not in control of any of them."*[12]

This falls a long way short, however, of letting go of everything completely. If prisoners harbour Hope for the future, then – as any survivor of the extreme elements will probably tell you – that Hope requires effort. Hope is meaningless if it is not put into practice through some positive, life saving act of self preservation, rather than succumbing to the powerful forces around you. Thrown into white water rapids, the passive floater risks being overcome, if not sent plunging over a waterfall; but the proactive swimmer fights the current.

In prisons, it is a constant struggle against the elements, because

---

10   Matthew Halliday, '*Bromley Briefings Prison Factfile*', (Prison
        Reform Trust, Winter 2019). P.12
11   Crewe et al. (2017), ibid, p.537
12   Crewe et al. (2020), ibid. p.125

the truth is – prisons save no-one, certainly not by design. At the final count prisons cause far more damage than they could ever hope to repair.[13] Instead of preparing people for life outside, they leave them largely de-skilled, de-socialised, and dehumanised.[14] The only real protection against the atrophy of mind, body and spirit in prisons is the strength of each individual's will, *"not just 'keeping busy', but being 'pro-active' in the development and pursuit of interests".*[15] That is, as Professor Ben Crewe and his colleagues explain: *"they have made decisions about their present actions that were orientated to a sense of who they wanted to be and how they wanted their lives to develop... to find some degree of hope, despite their exceptionally grim circumstances."*[16]

The desire to resist the ravages of time, the determination to confound and disprove the negative stereotypes and prejudices about what it is to be a 'prisoner', the strength to reject labels like *'offender'* or *'ex-offender',* and the self-belief that no glass ceiling – however strongly reinforced – is unbreakable. This is Hope in action, going against the grain rather than *'swimming with the tide'.*

Success like this comes in spite of being in prison, not because of it. Those who overcame the greatest obstacles in life all began their journeys with that same small flickering flame, a lighthouse across the ocean. The struggle to reach it through the storms and undercurrents is the story of Hope itself, and a testament to the human capacity for endurance and resilience.

---

13   Mark Alexander (2018), *'A Phenomenology of Freedom: Finding Transcendence in Captivity',* Journal of Prisoners on Prisons, 27 (2), pp. 54-74
14   Crewe et al. (2020), ibid. p.190
15   Ibid., p.173
16   Ibid., p.203

Train Delayed

By Annette de Jong

Don't you think the prison environment is akin to a busy railway station platform? A little hectic location, full of people scurrying here and there, always running a little late. The clattering metallic sounds of metal doors and key chains are punctuated by a tannoy announcing incomprehensible messages and instructions. The officers are the train guards bellowing last calls for meds and dinner, rather than chasing up the stragglers for the 9:28 train. But *your* train to Hopesville is delayed. Your journey has come to an abrupt stop.

You're going nowhere.

You sit and wait. You read a book, chat with your fellow waiting passengers. Will you take the same train as before this interruption to your journey, or will you cross to the other platform and take a different train, in the opposite direction? This time, just make sure you have a valid ticket.

They say the journey is more important than the destination, it's how your get there that is key, but was this station platform waiting room they call prison part of your journey?

When you plan a journey, you have a starting point. You take with you all the things you need and often overpack, just in case. You know your destination and you plan your route. There is a purpose to your journey. All journeys, both long and short, can be filled with a fizz of excitement - whether taking the bus, car, train or plane. Life's journey which brought you here to the prison platform is full of pain, misery and self-loathing. A daily cycle that spirals around and around. An out of body experience, out of your control.

My life's journey has had its highs and lows, like all of you, but thankfully nothing that was not insurmountable. For me the pain in my heart and the grief I was suffering which brought me here has now been exacerbated by the distress and fear the justice system has brought to bear. The system didn't want to ask me the most important of all questions, because the system more certainly did not want to hear my answer, which was the truth. The question of 'why did you commit this crime?' The system is not interested. Instead it will accept lies as gospel, without query. Heaven forbid you get a chance to speak the truth. You are gagged into silence.

Your silence helps the system, so it does not have to acknowledge you as a person. After all, people are complicated: it's a lot easier not to let you have your say. If the truth were spoken, your outcome may be very different from the one they have planned for you.

It is a system that erases possibilities as well as creating its own. It can convict based on what might have happened, rather than what did happen. For example, if you were driving a car at 30 miles per hour and had an accident, the damage would be less than if you drove faster. IF you had been driving at 70 miles per hour the damage caused would certainly be worse, of course, but you weren't driving at 70 - you were driving at 30. But you're convicted on the premise you COULD have driven at 70.

How does this make for a fair and balanced legal system? It

doesn't. All those who work or are involuntary part of the system know this to be the case. This sort of thinking by the justice system is good for their statistics and above all good for business. Ching-ching, £££££, we all have a price on our head. The entire system deals in people - we are the commodity. Could the justice system be construed as a modern day slave owner, from the money it makes from incarcerating people?

As a woman in this three-ring circus of chaos I can only gauge from what I have been told and my own experiences. Women are made an example of in the courts. Comparative or more serious crimes committed by men often draw a more lenient sentence. Why? There is sexual discrimination within our justice system, even by women judges towards women perpetrators. Society's opinion of women has much to be blamed for. We are known as the fairer sex after all. Society *expects* some men to behave badly. The view is that women are peaceful, demure, placid, and only behave in a respectful way. Yes we are and do, BUT we do have powerful emotions and like our male counterparts we do unleash them at times, often with devastating effect. Particularly when dragged down into intolerable situations within our lives, which are often caused by men. It is our positive behaviour traits that often hinder us, as the love and care we offer so freely is abused by others to create toxic, volatile and violent environments.

The law refuses to take on board that we all have outbursts of emotion which cause us to do things that are outside of our usual character. We all know right from wrong, but sometimes wrong is right. The justice system is black and white, with no time for emotional mumbo-jumbo. This is a strange irony in a system which deals with human beings. These primitive emotions make us all who we are; it's what makes us human. We are driven by our emotions; they drive our behaviour; they drive our journey. How can this vital human trait be ignored by an inert and stagnant justice system?

Are we not living in the twenty-first century, where we have a better understanding of human behaviour? Are we not more enlightened as to what makes us tick, so shouldn't we be using this accrued knowledge to offer an improved solution, rather than throwing everyone in jail? You've been sold a one way ticket.

I know for some this pause on the platform is an opportunity to get away from a dreadful situation, take stock, take a deep breath and prepare to move on once again. But not all of us need a cell in which to do this. Locking people in cages is a bizarre and primitive concept. Who benefits? Definitely not the prisoner, nor the victim and not society either. The law in the way it currently functions is failing us all.

Those I've met in this waiting room have been a real mixed bag. Some I have avoided, some I have been happy to chit-chat with. Then are those special passengers who have come into my life. Together we have shared our suffering. They have made me believe there is light at the end of the tunnel, even in my darkest of times. Unfortunately they will not be taking the same train; they have longer to wait.

One day my train will finally pull up at this bleak platform. I will have my ticket to Hopesville clutched tightly in my hand. The door will open and I will step aboard. All I can hope is that the next destination is a brighter, happier and more peaceful place.

In the meantime I sit in hell's waiting room.

So far this journey has been a torturous affair, blowing my entire world out of the water. I have been labelled with a luggage tag which declares to all that I am now a CRIMINAL.

Feeling like a piece of baggage, I just hope my next journey isn't to lost property.

The Ties that Bind

By L.J.T

No matter who you are, where you're from, or what your colour is, prison gives you time to think. Esau was no great thinker. Like many, his recreation was to let his TV play in a ceaseless loop of sitcoms, soaps and adverts as he sat on his bed in his skinnies eating cereal. Now he stood leaning on a rail overlooking the silent cellblock contemplating how he came to be there.

Each day he wakes, tidies, does push ups and sit ups, hydrates, then goes to work. Work is not easy to get when so many people have the same skill-set and are applying for the same jobs. Esau didn't stand out from the crowd academically - he hadn't taken to school and school hadn't taken to him. His employment history consisted of delivery driver and nightclub bouncer; neither enjoyable, both badly paid. Being spat on and swung at by drunk white boys was an occupational hazard. *'Had I got the job because I was black?'* he thought. *'Some sort of equal opportunities crap... huh, a young black guy in prison, I'm a walking cliche!'* He couldn't help smile to himself, but he knew, in the grand scheme, that he should be grateful for the cash it had brought.

The prison job he had now was simple enough. A ton of paperwork, and trying to help out inmates with their problems. Prison comes with its own unique world of problems. When he first arrived he'd been bewildered - it was chaotic and shit scary.

Day one Esau had experienced a problem he hadn't counted on. He'd been warned about avoiding crap from the natives but expected a better quality of guard than Mr Ackerman. A barrel of a man, as overweight as his ego, as short as his temper, a coarse beard and pug face as ugly as his personality.

"Another one of you lot" was the first thing he'd said to Esau. *"Just stay the fuck out of my way, don't talk to me or even look at me! You got that Darky?"*

Seriously, how do you reply to that? Esau felt heat rise up his back, the old anger ached his limbs, pulsing to break free. He'd had this a lot working as a bouncer and he'd been called a lot worse by bigger men than this jumped up prison guard. So, he'd clenched his fists and said *"Sir"*, then looked to the floor as Mr Ackerman turned his back and walked off.

Not wanting to rock the boat, Esau hadn't said anything to anyone, and he'd avoided Mr Ackerman ever since. The rest of the staff were decent people just getting on with their day jobs, which made life easier, but it was an incident Esau has not quickly forgotten

All these problems and he was supposed to help out others with theirs? Society teaches us to fix your own problems; even those paid to help tell you to *'sort it yourself'*. He'd seen a counsellor once - his mum had died young and dad left - so with all that baggage the counsellor had told him he had a lot of unresolved issues and pent up aggression. Really? No shit!

"Hey Boss!"

Esau turned from the railing as Sonny approached along the landing, *"sup Sonny?"*

"Boss, you heard anything 'bout my job yet? I asked agor, you know Miss Taylor? I asked her yesterday and she said she would ask, but you know she don't care nere."

"Yeah, no one loves you like I do Sonny". Esau smiled and knocked fists with him in respect. *"I've not heard anything but I'll ask around".*

Sonny had asked every day since he had applied for the cleaning job a week ago - him and six others.

"Yeah man, I know you're the one to get it sorted. I'll ask you again tomorrow alright? Don't you forget me now."

Sonny strolled off down the stairs, probably to accost anyone else he could about the job. Esau watched him go and shook his head. Sonny was more desperate to work than others here. It wasn't just the extra time out of cell; he had a girl and kid outside and he sent his allowance to them, meaning he lived in here with next to nothing. Not for the first time Esau thought that if he could, he'd help out every family on the outside; the people that really suffered, not the convicts but those left behind to pick up the pieces with a man-shaped hole in their lives. Not guilty of a crime but punished for being the wrong person. Esau shook his head again and went about his work.

***

Sepia light flooded the corridors, all drained of colour as afternoon turned to dusty twilight. Esau thought of his bed, telly and sleep as he walked the halls and deposited papers under cell doors. Then he heard shouting - the prison is full of noise. Orders from guards and cat calls of cons, but the pitch of fear and tremor of hurt in this shout sent Esau running. A cell on the top floor, its door slightly ajar. *"No!" "Stop!"* cried one voice, as another said *"shut it."* This was broken by a sound that reminded Esau of a butcher hacking into meat on a slab.

Stepping towards the door, Esau saw a guard bent over a curled up figure on the floor. The thumping sound he'd heard was that of a truncheon as it rose and fell, tenderising human flesh. Without hesitation Esau stepped forward.

"Hey! Ease off, he's down!"

The guard turned, stick raised, face flushed. *"Back off! I'm dealing with this."*

Mr. Ackerman growled as Esau looked to the whimpering figure of Sonny on the floor, who was attempting to crawl under his bunk.

"No, you back off! What's going on?" Esau demanded.

"Don't you dare question me! He went for me, I retaliated, now fuck off while I sort him out." Spit flew from Mr Ackerman's mouth and clung to his beard as he yelled.

Esau paused. It took the briefest of moments to weigh up the options of right and wrong and self-preservation.

"No," he said. *"You'll stand down or I'll go to the governor about this."*

"What? You're taking his side, are you? You gollys sticking together, is that it? You won't tell anyone or I'll see you lose your job." He jabbed his podgy finger into Esau's chest.

The anger flared as if Mr Ackerman had pressed a button, but he kept it down to asking the pressing question. *"Why didn't you sound your alarm?"*

"What?" Ackerman said, hesitantly.

"If you were attacked like you say, why didn't you hit your panic alarm?" Esau asked.

"I don't need help to deal with him."

"What will your body cam show, Mr. Ackerman? Will it show the attack?" Esau probed, suspecting the truth.

Ackerman paused. *"It's not on. The battery is dead, not that it's your business. Now fuck off or I'll do to you what I done to him, Darky!"*

Esau stepped forward. But instead of unleashing his rage, he felt it turn to ice - an anger just as powerful but harnessed to his command. Each word he spoke next carried more force than any punch he could throw.

"My name is Mr. Esau. You'll call me by my name and show me respect; we are the same rank. I don't care how long you've been here; you will not threaten me and you will stop hurting him."

Ackerman stood there in silence. Mr Esau pressed the alarm on his belt.

"Now, drop that stick." In the background came the thunder of running boots along the hall.

* * *

Mr Esau rode with Sonny to the hospital. All Mr. Esau could do was apologise for the hurt as he sat by his side.

"Don't you be sorry, boss," Sonny replied. *"You are just people, all you screws and us cons, we are just people. You know we are*

all in prison - I don't mean back there prison, I mean in our minds. Mine has always been drug addiction, Ackerman's was hate, and you got yours. It doesn't matter where our bodies are, we just gotta set ourselves free. Oh, and boss, about that job. I get it now, right?"

Mr Esau thought about what Sonny said when he finally got home to his cell of a cramped apartment. He'd carried his anger in him as his own prison. But today that all changed. Tomorrow he'd wake, breakfast, exercise and go to work, but he would not be in prison.

Twisted Path

By Stephen S

Ceri laid her head on the brown pub table, dreaming of another life, dribbling freely, arms dangling towards the faded blue carpet.

'Come on, sweetheart. Can't have you sleeping there before the lunchtime rush.'

Luke anxiously flicked his head over both shoulders looking for his boss. Ceri squinted up with half-open green eyes at his friendly smiling face full of concern, with his dark brown curly hair bouncing to attention.

'I'm fine, Luke. Another half a lager will keep me awake!' Ceri felt his strong fingers on her shoulders as he lifted her upright.

Luke sighed. *'I'll bring it over. I trust you!'*

Ceri watched him walk away and thanked God that Luke worked here. Not many blokes would give her this many chances without wanting something in return; and he didn't. She had offered herself on a plate so many times, but he had always been the perfect gentleman. Sadly, she had no hope with him.

'There we go, Ceri. Why don't you pop to the ladies and make yourself even more beautiful?'

'Okay, Luke. Thanks for understanding.' Her hand touched her limp straw-like blonde hair, sneakily sniffing her armpit as she did so.

'I don't mean to pry. You're so young but you're in here most days getting hammered. Why?' Luke eased himself on to the hardback

chair.

'Got nothing else to do, plus I meet all my mates in pubs.' Ceri could not bring herself to meet his sky blue gaze.

'Where are they then, Ceri?' Luke took no pleasure in saying that. It hurt them both. He walked away, head bowed, damp cloth dangling.

'Yo, Ceri! A voice that could chill ice cut through the bar.

'Cindy! Looking gorgeous as ever!' Ceri quickly rubbed her damp face.

'Why thank you, dear child. All natural, you know!' Cindy bellowed for two pints of strong lager as she stroked her flame-red hair.

'I thought you were going, Ceri?' Luke stared at her, eyebrows raised.

'No chance, matey! My best girl is here! All day session, babe?'

'Do bears shit in the woods?' Cindy kicked her purple padded jacket under her chair.

'What?'

'Don't matter. The answer is yes! I cleaned out the old man's wallet when he was in the shower. He won't notice until he tries to buy lunch!' Cindy sucked hard on her strawberry flavoured e-cig.

'How long you been married, Cindy?'

'Eight years.'

'Wow. You're only 28, babe.' Ceri watched as Cindy applied another layer of red nail polish.

'Got knocked up our first date. My dad "suggested" it would be a good idea to wed.'

'Why does your hubby put up with you?'

Cindy stood up and gestured to her body as she struck a pose. 'Look at me! Plus I am really loveable!'

Ceri knocked back her pint as Luke watched. He knew she was only 17 but he wanted to keep an eye on her. Keep her safe.

'I didn't know you had a baby, Cindy?'

'I don't. Month after getting hitched I lost it, but already had the ring heralded to my finger. Gutted.'

'Bummer. You always been faithful?' Ceri inhaled the fresh nail polish.

'Of course, but only because I don't count things that happened before I hit 21!'

Luke struggled to concentrate on his job.

*****

'What time is it, Ceri?'

'I think my phone is bust. It's all blurry. It's about 3ish.'

Ceri fell off her stool and Luke caught her just as her backside bounced for the second time. 'My hero! You are such a gent! Now take me upstairs to your room and ravish me!' Ceri launched her wet lips at his face.

'No, Ceri.'

'Why?' Ceri slumped to a seating position as she whined her one-word question.

'Because I'm 12 years older than you and I don't want to spoil our friendship.'

'You are way too nice to be real, man.' Cindy snorted into her lager.

'Thanks, Ceri, I'll take that as a compliment.' Luke threw Cindy a steely look.

'*It wasn't meant to be*,' Ceri playfully slapped his hard chest. Cindy and Ceri slammed open the pub doors and staggered up the street, giggling like a couple of toddles full of sugar.

*****

After his shift Luke went to another bar to relax. As he waited to be served Cindy weaved past him, bouncing along the wall, stuffing notes in her bra.

'*Where's Ceri, Cindy?*'

'*In the gents having fun. Not that you know what that is! Leave her alone!*' Cindy ran straight outside, letting the cold air in.

Luke hurried to the toilets with hardly a moment's hesitation. He could hear the tell-tale sounds from the cubicle that he had heard often enough in his own pub. There were three voices.

*****

Luke smiled stiffly when Ceri walked in the pub the next day. He had never seen her look so rough.

'*How are you this afternoon, gorgeous?*'

'*Ill. Was I in here yesterday?*'

'*Until you fell off your stool at about 3pm. Why?*'

'*It's weird, Luke. I really don't remember much about yesterday. I woke up this morning in a bush just off the High Street. Even for me that's bad. No idea what happened to Cindy.*'

Luke looked at her pretty face and felt so much pain. She was as delicate as a daisy petal. Just then Cindy walked in the door.

Luke grabbed her arm. *'I know what you are doing, Cindy'.* Luke hissed the words through clenched teeth sounding like an angry snake. *'You just keep robbing off your husband and stop selling Ceri and I won't say a word.'* Luke could feel his face burning and felt Cindy's arm tense as he refused to relax his grip. They stared at each other like a cat and a dog crossing paths unexpectedly. Cindy spun on her heels and left. No screaming. No shouting. Luke knew he had hit a nerve.

*****

Ceri came running up to Luke waving the local paper in his face. *'Look, look, it's in the paper!'*

'Slow down! Have you won another beauty contest?'

Ceri ignored him.

'Look! It's Cindy. She's been arrested for stealing from her husband! Can they do that?' Ceri's eyes flashed across the page.

'Sounds like he's had enough and wants to get rid of her or just teach her a lesson. Either way, babe, best stay out of it.' Luke felt a solid weight lift as he stifled an approaching smile.

'I am! I don't want to get caught up in that crap.' Ceri pushed the newspaper away. Luke noticed her sparkling green eyes and shining skin. Time away from Cindy had worked wonders and as he felt his heart pound like a galloping stallion, he realised how much he fancied her. *'See you soon, Luke.'* Ceri waved without looking, her voice smiling. He hoped she meant it.

*****

A few weeks later Luke heard on the barman's grapevine that Ceri had signed up for a Social Care college course.

'I hear congratulations are in order, young lady!'

'Eh?'

'College! Brilliant news! Champagnes, madam?' Luke was puzzled by her distracted expression.

'College? I've got more hope of winning the lottery. I'm pregnant but have no idea how. I haven't had sex in six months.'

Luke felt his stomach churn like an air-pocket drop on an aeroplane. His mind raced back a couple of months to that night in the pub toilet and Ceri with those two men.

'Ceri. I've got something to tell you.'

There was reluctance, a feeling behind his blue eyes that unnerved her.

'Do you remember that night you got hammered with Cindy and you woke up in a bush?' Luke could feel nervous sweat on his wrists.

'Sort of. Some of it, anyway.'

'Before you left this pub, me and you went upstairs and made love. When you didn't say anything about it, I guessed you regretted it and I was gutted so I haven't mentioned it.' Luke looked everywhere but at her.

Ceri was breathless. Her mind all mixed up like too many strobe lights exploding in her mind. *'You mean this baby is yours?'* Ceri's thoughts staggered as much as her feet.

'It must be. I'm really sorry.' Luke pulled his sweatshirt sleeves over his damp wrists.

Ceri launched herself at him and planted kisses all over his face and neck as she felt his arms lock tightly around her quivering body, making her feel alive and safe, just as she imagined love should be. *'I'm sorry I can't remember making love but I'm not sorry about the baby. Our baby. Not now I know you are the father!'* Ceri let out a cry which reminded Luke of a very excited kitten touching snow for the first time.

'I love you, Ceri'.

As her face refused to stop smiling, Ceri finally knew what it was like to be blissfully content. *'I love you too, Luke. Have you spilled something? Your wrists are soaking. Can you get me a lemonade, please?'*

Time Spent

By Adam C

A split-second decision can change everything. To remain lying in his mate's bed-bug infested flat, feeling weak, sick and craving heroin - or to get onto his feet, grab the knife from the kitchen and head out to the only shop open at 8 o'clock in the morning two days before Christmas to steal money and make himself well. The little devil inside his head is awake.

Deep within the brain lies the Amygdala, which stores and remembers pleasures experienced through our senses and creates an association within us. These pleasures are learned throughout our lives and our brains recall them and send us messages to indulge in them. This is called a craving. Jude was only in the shop for two minutes; that was all it took. Those two minutes would change his life. Jude was a drug addict: a lifelong heroin, cocaine and alcohol user. One substance alone was bad enough, but combine these and the potential for craziness is tripled.

Jude had dreamed of becoming a professional musician. From the age of fourteen, when he got his first electric guitar, Jude favoured growing his hair long, smoking cigarettes and being in a rock band over passing exams. The idea of fame and fortune and travelling the world on tour was more appealing than going to University.

Jude got his first job at age seventeen at Shendi Manor and Golf Club as a 'pot boy' (a glass collector), as it was known. It was here that he met Matt 'Mopi' Ireland, a barman who lived and worked at the complex. When Matt wasn't working, he liked to drink Diamond White Cider, smoke the odd spliff of hashish and listen to Motorhead. He had worked out a brilliant way to get free booze. Close to the end of a shift Matt would grab a few bottles of cider and beer, then lay them down by the outside cellar door. After he finished work he would walk around to the cellar and deftly snatch up the bottles. Nobody was any the wiser. Matt was the first person to introduce Jude to cannabis. It would become a daily ritual; it went well with the music.

In 1990, aged 25, Jude met Elsa Raucoules. Elsa stole his heart. She was from Pau, a small town in South West France, near the Pyrenees mountains on the border between France and Northern Spain. Elsa loved the English language and was keen on the literature too. She came to England and got a job as an au pair (nanny), with a family in Hertfordshire. Jude and Elsa spent all their time together that year and for Jude it was some of the happiest memories.

In October 2000, Jude went to live with Elsa in Bordeaux, France. Elsa went to university and Jude experienced a different way of life and culture. He loved it. They had a nice, big top floor flat in the heart of the city. Bordeaux had its fair share of music venues and Jude certainly absorbed plenty of them. Within a few months their relationship began to break down. Elsa had met someone else and asked Jude to move out. This would cause him heartbreak and sent him to find solace in drink.

In late 2001, Jude returned to the UK. He moved back to live with his father. The first few weeks were hard, but then he landed a job at Kodak, working in the office building catering department. Shortly after, he moved into a shared house not too far from work. The house he shared with four others turned out to be a party house; every weekend people would descend on the place to drink alcohol, smoke cannabis and snort cocaine. Within a few months, Jude was spending all of his wages on cocaine and it wasn't long before he started missing days at work. After several warnings from his employer, Jude was dismissed. Shortly after that he began attending meetings for substance users at the Turning Point charity for addiction. He moved back to his dad's for a while and focussed on his recovery with Turning Point. The cocaine use subsided but was to be replaced with alcohol, quite the contrast in psychological effect. The interest in music for Jude had waned, the drive to play live had diminished - until an encounter with an old friend and band mate from Jude's teenage years, Mark.

In 2004 he moved in with Mark and Andrea. By this time, he was working again and was meeting women. In his experience with the fairer sex, the majority wouldn't entertain excessive drinking and drug use. Jude's housemates during this time weren't so much into indulging in regular partying, which led him to use in secrecy and on his own. He found comfort in his own space with music and isolation.

Over the next few years Jude would move home several times and find a secure job working in a private school where he would stay for five years. The alcohol consumption would increase, and the reappearance of cocaine would occur. Jude enjoyed the job at the school and his fellow employees would also become his friends. During term time his attendance was generally consistent, but it was the long holiday periods that he would find a challenge in keeping himself occupied and off the drink.

In 2010, Jude entered rehab in Bury St Edmunds for ten weeks. Russell Brand, the comedian and Davina McCall, the TV presenter, had both recovered from their addictions at this treatment centre. So, in Jude's mind it was possible for him too. He did the work and engaged well with his mentors, attended lots of AA meetings and graduated after the ten weeks with his parents present at the celebration. His father drove him back to the place he was renting when he left for rehab; his landlord had kindly kept his room for his return. The familiarity and feeling that nothing had changed would remain cemented in his mind, which drove him to carry on drinking. Rehabilitation means 'to restore to former position' Jude wanted to get his life back, but didn't want it enough; it was easier to remain in denial and escapism.

In 2013, Jude was fired from the job at the school, which pushed him deeper into hopelessness. He got into hanging around with other people who were out of work and spent a lot more time drinking. It was around this time he would first try heroin. All drugs, including alcohol, have the potential to cause the recipient some problems but there is something more powerful in heroin and crack cocaine that can ruin lives.

Jude had found employment in a nice care home. He could walk to work and live at his dad's initially for a few months whilst he got back into the swing of things. Soon after starting the new job he met Hayley who was a senior carer at their workplace. They started a relationship and things seemed to be going well for Jude, but the heroin use increased. A few months passed and Jude had been sacked from the care home. He and Hayley had split. This sent Jude on a downer and he was using heroin and crack on a daily basis. Eventually, as the drugs were costing more and more, he failed to pay rent to his landlord and was evicted as result, leaving him homeless. In some cases, becoming homeless and on drugs can lead to a person resorting to crime.

In January 2016 Jude went to prison for the first time. He spent three months in HMP Bedford, then was released on license with nowhere to live. Between 2016 and 2020 he would be convicted four times, the longest four years and six months of which he is still serving in HMP Highpoint. One thing prison gives is time. Jude decided to use this time positively by educating himself. English, Maths and an Open University course. He would put in the effort and enthusiasm into his studies as he had done with obtaining drugs outside.

Prison is supposed to inflict punishment upon the person for their wrongdoings and to take away their freedom. This is true up to a point; for some it is an inconvenience to their activities outside and to others an opportunity to make positive changes to their lives. Jude took that opportunity to improve his own life and to believe that there is hope for him even when he makes those split-second decisions that can throw your life into turmoil.

Joint Enterprise

By Steve K

In January 2009 I was given a life sentence for murder under joint enterprise. I was blackmailed by my legal team to plead guilty in order to protect my six-week-old son from being taken into care, and to protect my fiancé from being given life also. I wasn't involved in the murder, or even in the room when it took place. She was in the room and was covered in blood. The CP's in Lancashire were going to say she was involved. Our son had had just been born (with her, in prison on remand) and I was taken to bond with him three weeks before my 'trial' began.

On the morning that the trial was due to begin I was eager to get it started, to prove my innocence, and to go home and begin our life as a family. I met with my QC, junior barrister and solicitor in the cell area of Preston Crown Court on the 30th of June 2008. My QC had to think of my partner and child - that if I ran a trial, she would get a life sentence and our son would be taken into care. I broke down and asked what I could do to stop that. I was told if I pleaded guilty, she would be freed and go home with our child. I was given just one hour to decide all of our lives and futures as a family. An hour later I pleaded guilty to a murder I didn't commit. Four days later I and the killer were given life sentences. I have not seen my beautiful boy since Blackpool social services got involved and said I was a risk to him. I am deemed low risk to children by the prison service and have no offences against any child on my records. From the day I was given the life sentence I've been fighting my 'conviction', as well as to see my son. I have now spent nearly thirteen years in prison for a murder I didn't commit. My son will be thirteen in April 2021. A family member of his told him when he was only nine years old that his dad is in prison, and for murder. He is now fearful of me.

In March 2009, just after my sentencing I was moved to my first of several lifer prison wings. I arrived at HMP Dovegate and was placed on a wing full of killers. From that day onwards I have resolved to *never* stop trying to prove my innocence, and to see my boy.

In April 2010 my appeal against conviction was heard in the High Court in London. It was refused, but Lord Leveson and two other judges stated I had left the flat with 'the murderer or murderers', i.e. *I am not the murderer*. I was broken that they had refused my appeal. My case then went to the CCRC for a review. It has been refused by them four times since 2010 and is currently back there now via new evidence. I have kept going for all of these years due to my unfailing love for my child and the burning injustice of my case. The junior council in my defence told me to 'think of Kieran' when blackmailing me to plead guilty.

There is a reason also that further gives me *hope*. In late 2010 I read an article about a new campaign group called JENGbA. They had been set up to support prisoners who are help on joint enterprise murder charges. Joint enterprise is a three hundred year doctrine that had been reissued to help tackle gang violence in Britain's cities. The head of JENGbA, Gloria Morrison and all her volunteers, have been helping over one thousand of us prisoners held on this monstrous doctrine. They have campaigned for us relentlessly for over a decade. In February 2016 they helped to force the Supreme Court (in JOGEE case) to say that joint enterprise had been misinterpreted for over thirty years, and that CPSS had taken a 'wrong turn.' Believing that all of our cases would be retrospectively reinvestigated we all believed in hope.

What we all then came to realise was that joint enterprise had now become politicised. The government and judiciary are fearful of the Supreme Court ruling. They are equally fearful of JENGbA as they are a voice for all of us. They also fear all of us from speaking out. In the four and a half years since the (JOGEE) ruling in the Supreme Court, only ONE prisoner has had his murder conviction overturned. It was replaced with manslaughter and he was freed on a time served basis. This means that he will receive no compensation for the years he served over what he would have done if he had been given an original sentence for manslaughter. The fact that he then went on to become a hero of the London bridge terror attack by foiling the terrorist by using a fire extinguisher I hope will now show the British public that those of us held in prison under joint enterprise might just have a great deal to offer.

Like my friend John Crilley, I have been held in many of our countries toughest prisons. I have had to reside in Dovegate, Longlartin, Gartree, Lowdham Grange, Swaleside, Berwyn and Preston. I have maintained my innocence *every day* I have been held. I have never engaged with courses that are designed for the guilty. Due to my stance I have been treated (or mistreated) like a dog because I refuse to earn HMPPS-MOJ money by doing courses that fail. I've had the tag of 'in denial' because I pleaded guilty. I have offered to take a polygraph test to prove I didn't kill the man who died and that I was blackmailed to plead guilty. Lancashire police refused, as did all of my former legal team.

In 2015, I suffered a severe stroke and heart failure that nearly killed me. It has left me in a wheelchair but I still *hope*. I have a solicitor who believes in me, and in my case. I have Gloria, and everyone at JENGbA. I have the truth on my side. I have stated I will *never* sign any parole document that would 'release' me on a life licence, as someone who didn't kill anyone. I either win my appeal and go home to my Kieran and I show him I love him, or I will stay in prison until my dying day.

I'm forty eight years old now and there is nothing that can be done to me, or taken away from me that will make me cease my fight for justice.

Becoming a Writer in Prison

By M.M

It's 2:47 am. You're normally asleep by 12:00. You know as you write a stanza and dream of a rose the door could crash open filling the room with aggressive prison officers. They'll strip you naked and watch you squat. You brush the thoughts aside like the scrap paper covering your wannabee masterpiece.

You think of your son. Is he safe? Dreaming of the dad who's been in prison for as long as he can remember? He's in college now. You think you should write him a letter. First you want to finish this poem about a rose.

You pass it to another aspiring writer. He's 10 years ahead of you, can tell his participles from his prepositions, but he's in for rape and it makes you feel uncomfortable.

You start to think about the mother of your child, your first rose. You met as children writing childish messages: *'R u in? B dere in 30 x.'* The street life gripped you so now you won't *'b dere'* for 18 years.

*****

You lay on your spiky prison bed once.

'Are you drunk?' you say down the phone.

'Yeah', she laughs. *'I can't find my friends.'* Her voice is strangely happy as if she has taken drugs or been spiked.

'Where are they?'

'Chatting to guys in the club. I can't find them.'

'Are you alone?'

'Yeah.'

Your eyebrows twist. Your lungs become annoyed. The empty night stares through the iron bars. Nineteen year-old petals, you think, shouldn't be wobble-leg intoxicated and alone in new cities.

'Do you want to go back to the hotel? We can talk on the phone if you do?'

'I'm going to get a taxi now.' The call ends.

As you wait you know the door could burst open – they'll strip you naked, steal your possessions, hurt you.

You phone her.

She cries. Without speaking.

'Rose, what's wrong?'

'I... I've been raped.'

*****

You look at the aspiring writer through fire red eyes.

'This poem is really good', he says.

You suppress the flames wondering how someone could jump out of nowhere and jump on the woman you love. It makes you want to jump out of nowhere and punch someone you don't really hate. But you don't believe in violence anymore. Your hands are for writing. You don't want to live with murderers anymore. Yet you always will: you live with yourself and the people you live with will live in your head forever.

You send the poem to the Koestler Awards. You don't win, but the feedback is helpful – you feel connected to the outside world. You tell yourself that your next piece is going to blow their minds. It will be about a big, beautiful rose that couldn't be harmed anywhere it went. Its thorns were made of instantly killing poisons and its leaves and flower were made of diamonds.

You cry on the paper. You feel like a wilting rose and know you're dying. You're in good health the doctor writes on a screen. Your heart rate is low, and your blood pressure is great. You write about a doctor who is lying. How can your health be good when you live in hell?

You tell him to check your mind. 'It's fine,' he says, like everybody else. But that's because you're lying. You're not crazy enough to say you're really crazy, so conform like the rest of the crazy world.

The diamond rose with poisonous thorns didn't win an award, yet it got kind feedback.

You begin to write a poem about an ordinary flower. It didn't know it was a rose and grew up in a tiny plot of soil outside an impoverished terraced council house. It was fragile, almost without leaves, and few people saw its beauty. You know it's a crap rose and a crap poem that no one will love, but you're depressed and tired so post it to the Koestler's anyway. Alongside some masterpieces.

You win an award for the crap rose poem. You start reading about the avant-garde, throw most of your possessions away feng shui style, and spout awful clichés, such as *less is more*. At least, you pray that every rose in the world is kept safe.

You fall asleep with a pen in your hand and the door closed hoping it opens at 08:15 and not before.

Prison Psychology & Other Practices

By L.D

Part 1

So, imagine someone has grabbed your hair and shoved your head in a bath of cold water. Slowly drowning you but at the last minute you are dragged onto a chair and instantly someone else forces a gun into your mouth. The terror in your eyes is duly noted before a black hood darkens your world. I am then left alone, until the next day when someone else arrives. But this time they tell me they are my friend.

He takes my hand and leads me outside into the light and takes off my blindfold. We head into a maze, like the one at Hampton court, but it's ten times bigger and five times higher. My friend leads me deeper in, telling me it will be ok. Eventually we arrive at the bit in the middle. This is when he flies away, leaving me alone, confused and disorientated. I have to make my way out, but how can I, when I am totally lost? Fear starts to creep in; too many blind alleys, the wrong path too many times. Every now and then I see my friend flying overhead, but he doesn't look down, even when I shout and scream. I try so hard to not let that affect me, but it does, because betrayal hurts. I continue looking, searching for a way out. The faces and shapes mock me. Eventually my searching turns into wandering aimlessly. Hope has turned to despair; a cold heart-breaking, meaningless existence.

After many years, and unknown to me, I've wandered close to the exit and this is where I meet another friend. I am so happy. She takes my hand and tells me she knows the way. Deep down I am very hurt by what has happened, and this has made me naïve. My new friend has led me back to the middle and back where I had started, and she also flies away. I feel something wet, I look down and see I have pissed myself. Traumatised, I stumble back out into the maze, lurching and swaying like a mental patient. Physical abnormalities and disease occurs. My crippled and twisted psyche senses it. I know a tumour is beginning to grow inside me. My legs become numb, causing me to collapse to my knees. The screaming starts and then stops after twelve days. I begin to rise and notice the hair in my hands, that I ripped in clumps from my head. I rub the hair into my eyes and blindly move forward. And moving forward, I am not looking for what isn't there. I know I will always be denied the joy of walking through the exit. Too many forces at play. The best I can hope for is my trap door, which could lead up or down.

Part 2

Someone clever once said: *"To find the wolves, don't look where they might be, look where they have been."*

I've always had a thing for wolves, mythological beings roaming the earth in packs. Hungry, relentless, careful and intelligent.

Animalistic purity. So, what does hope mean to me? Knowing that I will go and go and go and my destiny awaits.

Hope, Freedom and What it Means

By Ubaid R

Togetherness is a spell which can never be broken,
Community is the magic which none can compare.
Dream together collectively,
So that we can all get through this fear.

Hope, Happiness, Wish and Tranquillity
These are the magic beans
To give us a brighter day
We can see together, as a team.

Group, Collectiveness, Togetherness and Team
For words rarely used
Just to describe what "we" mean.

Morning sunshine cares, Happiness blooms,
The violet velvet petals of a flower,
Flourish as the various colours do too.

The gentle wind blows across my face
As each moment cares to pass.
Reminding myself keenly, that like every difficulty,
This slight wind will also come to pass.

Stay strong, maintain hope
The instructions are clear
Hold onto and care for life
As it is to me and everyone so dear.

Hope provides us all with some type of scope,
A lense to look through,
To help us strive, thrive and survive.

It's the key to our engine,
Of life, hope and aspiration.
It's the key to our lock
Invisible and hidden to everyone else.

Opening up for us
Mountains of treasures
Which no one else can reap from.

It provides us all with residency,
A means to go on.
It turns a rock-solid heart of strife into pure,
Valuable gold, all in one.

Climbing up the sturdy mountain top,
Accompanied by a passionate heart
Which just won't stop!

Determination!
Resiliency!
A motivation to go on.

Continue and carry on your path
To rediscover the greatness within you.
The potential, the drive, which lets you continue
On and on.

This is not just a simple rhyming rap sheet
NO!
These are the ingredients to provide you
With the means towards a successful result.

FREEDOM!
There I come! Running at you!
Nothing to stop me but the thin friction of air
While I come running at you.

Heart racing.
Pulse quick.
Nerves on edge.

"Blessed is your being!"
I scream at you
As I hurl my way out the exit gates.

Did I realise before your golden worth?
When you silently were in my life?
For so long, before, not complaining.

Come to me, here I am!
On my knees, pleading and begging for your mercy.
Beautiful! You are
Having travelled so far, to get to you, eventually
To the shining face of freedom.

With no restraint, no complaint.
There you are.
Just waiting there patiently
To re-enter into my life.

Freedom.

* * *

I'm Not Afraid

I'm not afraid of the empty walls which surround me
Screaming to me hollow sounds of unrest.
I'm not afraid of the black and bloody finger marks
Enlaced across the three walls to signify the test.
I'm not afraid of the corny pillow
Filled with sharp twigs, to rest on, and willow.
I'm not afraid of the harsh screeches
Coming from the neighbours next door.
Most nights when it happens
I end up terrified, petrified, curled in a ball on the floor.
Sickening! Maddening! Pure insanity
Cos of where I am as I look at all the four walls.
Where! To go? How! To see? Future! To be?
Me! To remain as me?
Tick tock! Goes the clock, the sound resonating against the walls.
Empty. Hollow… is all but the floor.
To walk on. Feel trampled. Under hooves. Feel stamped on.
Where? To go? The glancing, outside, goes on and on.
Just like the length of the horizon.
I'm not afraid.

I Was Nothing At All

Nathan E

The moon shined bright one warm summer's night. It was a sudden swift birth, my mother would say, when I came into the world on the twenty-first of May. The middle of three things were far from glee, slow to talk but quick to cry - tears all day, tears all night. There's nothing wrong, the tests would show, why he cries we just don't know. Try not to worry, the doctor would urge; he's just a baby who like to be heard. In time he will change, my dad told my mother, but for many more years I only talked to my brother.

As a toddler I explored, always curious and eager, allowing the world to come oh so nearer. I loved the wilds of our garden, thick and overgrown, so many wonders yet to be known. I formed a friendship with neither boy nor girl, but rather the creatures that blessed this world. The more unappealing to others the more I loved. Insects, spiders and other such grubs. For there is beauty in all; we must look past the warts, scales and hair. In the eye of the beholder such attraction will be seen, surely that's what makes us human beings?

As a young boy my interests had grown, and to other children it was starting to show. Teachers at school thought me quite strange, and other boys wouldn't let me play their games. But I didn't care if they thought me odd, for I would disappear to look for toads and frogs. Little did I know things were about to change, and the world as I saw it would never be the same. An older boy, stronger too, got close to me and our friendship grew.

It wasn't to be long before said friendship was changed, as the older boy began making demands. I soon came to realise he wasn't really my mate. I couldn't look in a mirror without shame or disgrace. The things I was made to do, I didn't quite understand, but I didn't dare say no when he grabbed my hand. Humiliated, torn, innocence shattered, it suddenly felt as though nothing mattered. Try as I might to run and hide, I couldn't escape the heartache inside. The abuse continued, it felt like an eternity, but the truth did surface, eventually. My parents were told; I could see the hurt in their eyes, which filled with tears as they looked up to the sky. The teachers at school also now knew, of the years of abuse I had gone through. They could only say sorry as they spoke of their grief. As for my abuser, he was left for the police.

Time moved forward and with that came a new school but still I would learn that people are cruel. True I was distant and my trust wasn't there; to many on the outside, it would seem I didn't care. I was just trying to heal, but the pain was to return and be all too real. For almost five years, I was beat black and blue - the reason, they told me, was simply 'we don't like you'. Stones, spit and bricks were frequently launched, along with the same old taunts. Eventually I alone was not enough for them to loath; my family were targeted, as well as our home. No matter what measures were put in pace to make change, things it would seem always stayed the same.

Over time I retreated, into loneliness and seclusion; my mind became warped with both anger and confusion. I hid from the word as I grew emotionless and cold; my voice grew bitter, solemn and old. I pushed those away who only wanted to be near - was it due to anger, distrust or fear?

Eventually came the voices. Sometimes kind, sometimes mean; a body to accompany them was yet to be seen. Soon came with demands, threats and false hope. This anger, I soon realised, targeted myself. I became paranoid and flooded with mixed emotions, like an ever-rising and ever-falling tide. I slipped further off the rail, attempted suicide, only to fail. Soon I was medicated, monitored and watched.

Past my twenty-first, Christmas that same year I was demobilised in fear. A secure hospital would be a temporary home. Schizophrenia, they said, a form of psychosis. PTSD, depression as well. My life, it would seem, had become pure hell.

And the list only got longer. Asperger's, autism and personality disorder. Who is this, I asked, banging my head against the wall. Perhaps I was nobody, nothing at all.

Medication brought change, both mental and physical. I soon gained weight, it happened very quickly. They told me politely that the anti-depressants were likely; the reason behind why I'd grown so unsightly. A decision was made, gradual of course: mental illness, I vowed, will not win this war! I went to college - art came first, then animal care and management. Soon I would look after animals – unwanted and unloved. My devotion to them would not come undone. I also pursued art, with many pieces being successfully sold. 'An idle mind was the devil's playground' - this I abolished, with work I was proud.

Matters were to only improve. I tackled my weight and bettered my mood. Eventually, something came that I thought would never be; another person told of their love for me. Said person had taken hold of my soul, as I soon felt love forever to hold. We made a life that was good and benefitted us both. Then came a day in May where I decided to go out.

Rarely did I ever venture out alone but what harm could come? I went to a bar, not planning to stay long, but soon a complete stranger started wagging their tongue. I didn't say much, that was usually my way; talking to strangers was not my forte. I felt awkward, loose and very uneasy. Things only got worse when they started to tease me. Time was moving on and I thought it best to leave, but I was followed as I stepped into the street. Matters became complex and I didn't know what to do. I wanted to say *leave me alone*, but I just didn't know how. Then came advances, of which I rejected, and aggression that was quite unexpected. No longer did it seem the situation could be managed. Familiar voices scratched at my head and before I realised it one of us was dead. Panic ensued with no rational thought; things only got worse when I made no report. There's no point in lying, I tried to hide what I'd done. I felt shame, fear and angst all at once.

Of course, it all came to a head, I expected it so. There was nowhere to run, nowhere to go. Arrested, charged and held on remand, then back to a secure hospital as assessments were planned. Specialists and doctors were in high demand, as I met plenty of patients who could only talk with their hands. The time did then come, as I left the hospital gates, whereby I returned to prison to await my fate.

Soon came the rumours and lies, all the tall tales that fuelled newspaper sales. Stories of horror and macabre fascination would be raised in an attempt to secure my damnation. I had about given up, I no longer cared, for I had lost all that I loved, my life was laid bare! My home was seized, all my belongings too. What happened to my animals, nobody knew? For fifteen years some were under my care; now they were gone and I didn't know where. My partner too, the love of my life, struggled to come to terms with what happened that night. For almost eight years we were never apart. I couldn't help but feel I'd broken their heart.

It all proved too much - the headache, the pain; life I knew would never be the same. Back to the start of misery, I had come so close to building a dream. Pain and sorrow were back yet again; it was all beginning to take quite a strain. My weight was to soar; alone in my cell, I was living my own private hell. Self-harming at times, of which I was prone, was one way to cope with my twenty-two stone. All of these struggles are my cross to bear, and although I don't show it, I assure you I care. For I deeply regret what happened that night; no one is deserving of losing their life. The guilt will stay with me and that I deserve. I'm sorry to those of whom I have hurt.

Regardless of how, when or why, there will come a time when I too will die. In death, I hope I am given wings, so that I can reach the heavens in the sky. As I search for an angel, of which I must plea, how sorry I am; can you ever forgive me? For I wanted not what happened that night, such anguish to occur where you lost your life. Once my message is heard, my wings will be taken, for there is no peace in heaven for those who are forsaken.

And so I will plummet, tumble and fall, to a place of which I have been before. As the pit was too open, ready to greet, I could feel the hot ambers burning my feet.

Who awaited, I asked? What was in store? Perhaps, like me; nobody, nothing at all.

Better than Most

By Essjae

In HMP Warren Hill I have found my best self
Why? Because of my safety I am much more certain
When I'm walking around this Suffolk establishment
I'm a lot more comfortable and don't feel as nervous

Thinking back to my stays in the bear pits
When I was looking over shoulders and peering out of curtains
Looking out toward the exercise yard
Seeing another con injured, thinking 'man, he didn't deserve it'

I heard murmurs of potential trouble on exercise
So the fact it kicked off makes me glad that I swerved it
Those warzones aren't so carefree, the rem 'eggshells' springs to mind
So it's understandably why some embrace the life of hermits

I knew these populations were too restrictive for growth
So the idea of a therapeutic community became more pertinent
I followed out the application for Warren Hill TC
And in 2016, I packed my kit and made the elongated journey

The moment I arrived I felt terribly at ease
Aided by the officers' shirt colours, which I thought was quirky
The Custodial Managers' t-shirts were a weird light blue
And the therapy officers adorned the colour of burgundy

Some staff were very forward, checking if I was alright
But coming from the jungles I found this rather unnerving
I became very anxious when realising the expectation
Which was to build up a strong relationship with my keyworker

Still , this was easier than being amongst hyenas and lions
Silverback gorillas, king cobras and serpents
Like anywhere, you can't get away from the moles
But although they might tell tales they won't physically hurt ya

A few of the men scream, "I'm not feeling this gaff!"
Because of a few minor dislikings but nowhere is perfect
Some don't like the fact that vulnerable inmates have a voice
But who are we to make any human feel worthless?

Yes, at times I've called this spot the psychological fryer
But the places previously were like the physical furnace
Some of the guys boast they'd love to return to them zoos
But when offered the chance they seem to always spurn it

When the conditions aren't optimal the flower can't grow
So not until I came Warren Hill could I start my resurgence
Every jailhouse liked to promote the word, 'Rehabilitation'
But in most vicinities, it's voiced with commas inverted

I'd like to thank Simon Davis for funding the Butler Law course
As I became part of the HMP and Cambridge merger
Where prisoners were tasked with producing advice guides for prisoners
Which helped us become half professional mini-researchers

And now it's leading to even grander prospects on release
Cambridge University opening its doors to life sentence servers
This'll lead to better relations between us and the community
Hopefully, with them helping us to educate and also vice versa

Inside here, so many opportunities have presented themselves
Making it impossible to remain in a state of inertia
You can be an artist, poet, musician or actor
And showcase in front of visitors who mainly come on Thursday

Said events are held, often in the chapel area
Which on weekends is safeguarded and basked in church hymns
But it is a multi-faith space throughout the rest of the week
And supports any faith or occasion that you'd have heard of

It too stages theatre in conjunction with Red Rose Chain
Open to residents but you have to be a studious rehearse

Those involved are having the time of their jail lives
Riding these gigantic creative waves like a surfer

In a prison where health and education are celebrated too
You can be a long-distance runner or a distance learner
You can get stronger and fitter in a well-equipped gym
And there's a decent amount of CV if you're a fat burner

11-a-side football on Friday afternoons
If you can dribble past defenders and bend in a pearler
It reminds me of the goal that I scored last season
When I played a quick one-two and the finish was unerring

The Saturday mornings are demarcated for Park Run
9 o'clock start on your marks no earlier
A slight snag in that there's no sports hall for racquet games
In a game of tennis, I'm like the world's best returner

Those not into sport or the arts, may be in academia
Students have got university assignments stockpiled on the server
And age ain't nothing but a matter of a number
Cuz at just 27, very few match the certificates of 'The Herbster'

I spend my existence mapping out things clear
I'm in my cell like Benedict in an episode of Sherlock
With the vast amounts of openings, I can't regress
I'm saying no to spice and that homemade Smirnoff

My type of night out, a big radio fight in Madison Square Garden
With a can of KA and half a pack of Werther's
I'm not too into the singing programmes like the X-factor
That's no disrespect to Simon and you know I love Dermot

In quiet I'm trying to plan my easy to a Stage 3 visit
Family in a nice private room with a fresh hot burger
A return to family remains the highest priority
So every day I reduce my risk with this as the purpose

Strangely, even though many of us are nearing our parole dates
This place is filled with some serious long termers
But the upside of this is that time's moving quickly
And many of the clients are in the final furlong

Which may not be as sweet as it was before
As there are measures for Warren Hill to introduce ROTL excursions
But just like the prison shop it won't be open to the TC, because like
Staff say, we're here to do therapy
Once we've completed, then we'd have earned it

If I progress from TC and PIPE, next is the Progressive Regime
However, those buildings are badly in need of a big refurbish
But even with these gripes, here is better than most
With an uninterrupted core day and so much fewer searches.

A Beautiful Thing

By Kody M

My name is Kody and what I'm about to tell you is a real account of my life and how hope has become a friend. Who I am is simple; what I am is complicated, being that I am bi-polar and a paranoid schizophrenic, but someone's opinion of me does not have to become my reality. I come from a broken home and suffered some sexual abuse, got myself into wrongdoings such as becoming a prolific drug taker, and into more crime. But I have faith in God and always hope that tomorrow the sun will shine on me.

You see, I should be dead. I've been self-harming since I was fifteen and taking overdoses. I nearly went into a coma at one stage when I took 110 ten milligram diazepam and cut my arm with a machete. I must have tried to take my own life about a dozen times, including overdosing on heroin to the point of having to be resuscitated by paramedics. But I'm still here and I'm here for a reason. I thought my reason was my beautiful boy - C.J, as we call him. But me and my ex-partner did not get on and I wasn't allowed to see my beautiful boy and I ended up on drugs again and very suicidal. I've been on every type of drug going: weed, ecstasy, wizz, heroin, crack, cocaine, L.S.D. You name it, I've tried it and I am not proud of it.

So many battles I have had with myself and given up but then hope comes back. You see, I have had darkness all around me, but never within me. Light over darkness, always. I got into sports when I was not on drugs; like I said - I am complicated. I had my first debut Thai fight organised twenty years ago and my best friend died of a heroin overdose five days before I was due to fight. I couldn't hold it together and broke down and fell into a million little pieces. Five years later I fought at a top venue and I won. But then more of my mates died from drugs and it hurt me loads and loads. I eventually got into unlicensed boxing white collar and did well; I only lost one bout which was a total miss-match.

Hope has always been with me all the way; hope has made me realise tough times don't last but tough people do. Hope can be bigger than my circumstances. So here I am once again in jail, the last time it was 28 years ago, and I'm back with hope again. You see, I haven't been allowed to see my beautiful baby son for two years, even though I am on the birth certificate - and oh boy the pain has killed me. Because my relationship broke down and I wasn't allowed to see him, I got back on drugs and became unhinged. I don't hate my ex, I don't hate anyone; I'm forgiving her because that's power; in fact I'm forgiving everyone that has ever done anything negative to me so I'm free and not a puppet on a string.

I have 12 months to serve and for the first time in 3 years I feel free, full of hope and the holy spirit. Having hope has transformed me and I believe a path has been laid out for me. I am being as productive as possible with my time. Once out of jail I intend to box again and fight for charity, in particular for the Clarendon Wing at the L.G.I in Leeds - it's a ward for kids who have cancer. I don't want credit or anything; it's what I'm meant to do.

I'm struggling with mental health, drug addictions, break ups, losing loads of mates to drug addictions and I'm still more steadfast and full of hope. So whoever you are, no matter what trial and tribulations you are going though, don't ever let go of hope. Anything is possible at any time in your life. Don't listen to the naysayers who have written themselves off. Hope is a very beautiful thing and more powerful than you can imagine - so get out there and live the dream.

p.s. I "hope" they haven't forgotten my polo mints for my canteen, ha-ha. Embrace hope everyone.

Hope In A Darkroom

By Spencer Y

I had heard it many times before, the story of how my mother died. Told by Kennedy, a.k.a. my father. He would tell it the most when he was drunk. "Your mother, my lovely wife, that you killed when you were born, we were childhood sweethearts you know."

I always used to think "*I didn't kill her, I never chose to be born and cause the death of my own mother during labour.*" But I knew that voicing these thoughts would be suicidal, because not only was Ken abusive verbally, he had also been abusive physically.

From the outside we seemed pretty normal: me (Sarah), my older brother Junior and the man the universe gave as my father - Ken, Kennedy... one more K and he would have fitted nicely in with another KKK. The man was pure evil. My older brother Junior was fine in the beginning; I learnt a lot about mum from him. What made her laugh, her favourite colour; you know, the things I couldn't learn from photo albums. I had always lived my life with a deep sense of guilt. I would think "*I killed mum, ME*"- but looking back now, I could see that my young mind had been polluted with propaganda.

My bedroom was a funny place really. On one hand I could watch all my programmes in peace, surrounded by posters of all my favourite girl bands, hoping one day I would travel the world with them. But on the other, it was a darkroom; the sort of place the devil would like to frequent with all his mates. So it was a safe haven during the day but a prison at night. I always wondered why nefarious activity flexed its muscles when Mother Sun returned home after a hard day's work. Most crimes are committed at night – DARK! The lighting in a nightclub - DARK! The mind of a nine-year old girl being abused – DARK!

Nine has now become my favourite number. Odd I suppose, since it was the age that it all started. But I still like the number nine because you can turn it upside down and make a completely different number: six. I like the thought of turning one thing into another. So, I now tell myself: "be a nine, be a nine" - turn your tragedy into triumph, but a tragedy it remained. Ken coming home from work, angry at life and bitter because he was the sole provider for two kids. It would start with Mr Jekyll, so he would ask me and my brother how school was, prepare dinner for us and generally be Quite (capital Q) decent. As he racked up the beers – Stella, to be precise - Mr Hyde was bubbling underneath. I could always discern the exact moment this metamorphosis was taking place; it was when he started to play his sad songs, the ones he used to say reminded him of my mother. Then he would stay something like: "Junior, why aren't you like daddy? You don't like football, you don't like boxing, I hope you're not gay." Laughing and slurring at the same time as he spoke, a skill only Ken had, and it was my cue to leave the arena.

I would go into my room, pick up a book and start to read. I was told mum loved to read; she could read a whole book in a day – well, that was what Junior would tell me. If that was the case it would have made her a very intelligent lady, someone who definitely would not have had children with a man like Ken. Going by some of the pictures of my mum and Ken when they first met, I believe he had allowed Mr Jekyll to be the only side she saw, because they looked so happy. He must have kept Mr Hyde in the boot and left him there for many years. But that's the problem with leaving a demon buried so long: when he is finally resurrected, the havoc on others is all the more intense.

At the time I used to think "poor Junior", because he didn't have a TV in his room like me so had to use the one in the living room. So if his team were playing on the telly, he had to watch them while being goaded to come out of the closet by his own father. Strangely Ken hardly hit Junior; he would hit me more. Probably he was scared that one day Junior would become big and strong when grown and have the ability to crush his little man frame. Plus with me he just saw my mother; she had green eyes, and so did I.

When the music went off, I knew the one-man party was over. Junior would be sent to his room and told to go to sleep straight away, since he had school the next morning. My super-sonic hearing would kick in, listening, waiting for Ken's drunken stagger to reach my door. For a man who had drunk more alcohol than a bar could hold, he was extremely delicate and light fingered whenever he opened my bedroom door.

Throughout the years of this ordeal, my books provided a much needed light in that darkness. I would hope and dream that one day I could visit the places I had read about. Telling myself that anywhere was better than here. The knowledge of the fact that I could leave that place when I turned eighteen drove me to persevere. I vowed the family I hoped to one day have would never resemble anything like mine.

* * *

"It's a girl, Sarah, it's a girl!" shrieked Rodney. "What shall we call her?"

Tears of joy rolled down my face and I stared into the child's green eyes. "Hope."

That was the name I gave my first child. Exactly six weeks later, I heard that Ken had been killed in a car accident. There was my favourite number again, turning life on its head.

Years later, with three beautiful kids (one girl, two boys), a loving partner and becoming the managing director of a charity that provides support for victims of abuse, the universe wanted to remind me that love always wins. When my nine-year-old daughter turned to me and asked "Mummy, why did you call me Hope" I turned to the apple of my eye and said "Mummy wished a long time ago that one day she could be a little girl again."

"A little girl again, Mummy? How?"

"Through you, Hope," I replied. "Through you."

Sounds Around Me

By D. L

It was 2017 and the first time Matt had ever been to a prison, despite the fact he was on remand and not convicted of any crime. It was a slow and staggered process moving the few belongings he had with him to the reception desk. An officer waited with a file on it, who proceeded to ask Matt his name, age and other details. They take a photo, then ask him the most stupid question of all: *how do you feel?*

After being brought to prison for the first time for a crime you haven't done, how are you expected to feel? Whatever your answer makes no difference anyway, as it's not like it will give you a 'get out of jail free' card.

So Matt moved to the holding cells while others are processed in a similar way. After about an hour, he is called up to be searched and issued with prison items: bedding, clothes, soap, a shaving kit, and a little faded booklet that describes the regime, apparently written by someone learning English. Then it's back to the holding cells to await medical and the 'induction.'

While in the holding cells, the conversation flows back and forth – small talk to ease jarred nerves, mostly. With the rattling of keys, it comes to an abrupt stop. Those keys go right to left, then back again, as guards take people from the other holding cells to their destinations. It's this locking sound that is lodged in the mind of every prisoner – an incessant chorus that lasts day and night, a reminder of being incarcerated even when you close your eyes. Eventually, Matt's name is called and he's summoned to see the nurse. She is a pretty brunette, perhaps in her mid 30s, and she goes about taking Matt's weight and blood pressure. Then comes that annoying question again: *'how do you feel?'* Matt just smiles and says he is doing fine. He wonders what she would say if he conveyed how he really felt. Back to the induction room, he is asked to complete a form about the prison rules. Then come more questions: *'Do you want to live with the main prison population of on the vulnerable prisoner wing?' 'Do you have any religious preferences or needs?' 'Do you want to make a phone call?'* For some reason, it's the religious preference question that seems to stick with him.

Being admitted to jail with no trial and getting asked about your religion – was it some kind of twisted joke? He had spent less than an hour receiving legal advice on how to get out of jail and argue his case, yet here he was in prison being asked what religion he followed. It would have been more helpful to receive advice on how to hire a good Legal Aid solicitor to help with remand and prepare for a jury trial.

Matt thought more about the question. Is there such a thing as God; did he create all human beings? By the time Matt was eleven years old, his knowledge of religious education could have earned him an A* at GCSE and probably A level standard due to him being brought up in a moderately organised Christian organisation. One of Matt's first books was a collection of bible stories. It covered the major stories of the Old and New Testaments, starting with the creation of the earth. It told stories of Moses speaking to a burning bush and parting a sea so he could lead the Israelites. It spoke of how when some angels left heaven, they took wives on Earth and their children became giants, or Nephilim, which caused God to cause the great flood. Noah was described, with his great Ark that carried two of each animal, was described to exodus, it told of when angels left heaven and had some wives on earth and their children became giants or Nephilim which God cleared up by flooding the whole planet, but not before instructing Noah to build a large vessel called an Ark to save two of each kind of animal. There were stories of Job, who was tested with trials and tribulations that made prison alone seem not so bad.

Through Matt's religious upbringing, he developed an aptitude for reading from the Bible, in turn helping with his writing. Though there were aspects of the religion he struggled with, he attended religious meetings three times a week – one hour on Tuesday, then two hours on Thursdays and Sundays. These meetings helped develop sharp time keeping skills, with many times Matt counting down the minutes until he could go home. All year round, he learned about the Christian calendar and effects on people in the organisation. Birthdays were not celebrated because a number of bible characters were killed on their birthdays, like John the Baptist and King Solomon. Christmas was also not recognised, because it was thought to be linked to paganism not actually the birthday of Jesus Christ.

Growing up, Matt had not appreciated the Christian organisation.

However, being older now, he continued to learn about all aspects of life. He watched as members, who claimed to be following the bible's rules and messages, took different paths. There was Dave and Rita – a seemingly happily married couple, until Dave left Rita and became an alcoholic. Then there was Sonya, who was exiled for adult activity outside marriage, caught on camera. Some took more extreme journeys: one ended up going to prison – and now there was another.

While study of any religion allows you to develop skills, it is clear that the Christian ideas have been greatly adopted as a form of teaching and control. A week after Matt's induction, he was in the prison chapel and being asked when God created Adam and Eve by a fellow inmate. Across from him, someone shouted over an answer: "about 6000 years ago". This is contrary to Darwin's theory of evolution, Matt wanted to say. It did not make sense for the world to be a few thousand years old when there was evidence of early humans from over 10,000 years ago, to say nothing of dinosaurs. It reminded Matt of the same debate that caused the elders of his religious organisation to run out of things to say.

In prison, inmates turn to religion for a wide variety of reasons - some good, some bad. People could learn ways of unity and peace, as well as getting an opportunity to spend their time better than being locked in a cell. Alongside this there was radicalism and groups who used the chapel to deal drugs or just as an opportunity to chat with people they knew on others wings. In spite of this, the idea that we are all connected in a spiritual way was powerful, bringing us to think of things greater than ourselves, and finding hope in God.

Definition of God:

1. *Spirit or being, worshipped as having supernatural power.*
2. *Object of worship of idol.*
3. *God in monotheistic religions - the supreme creator and ruler of the universe.*

Man's Quest for Meaning & Survival

By Terry S

One of the most draconic prison sentences in British criminal justice history for a non-fatal offence is the Indeterminate Sentence for Public Protection ('IPP'), introduced under Section 225 of the Criminal Justice Act 2003. The sentence was enacted on 4th April 2005 by David Blunkett MP of New Labour and abolished under the powers of the LASPO Act 2012, but unfortunately not retrospectively. Ultimately, those that were already serving IPPs were forced to complete their sentences.

It is emphatically argued that IPP is a form of internment. The definition of internment being detention without trial or keeping someone incarcerated for a crime they have yet to commit. The former Prison Governor John Podmore described IPP as a predictive sentence where *"We're locking them up not for what they've done, but for what they might do in the future".* [17]

Similarly, the incarceration of IPP prisoners can be compared and contrasted with the inherent hopelessness and uncertainty found in the horrific internment of Jews and others in the concentration camps of Nazi Germany between 1942-1945. As a consequence of this previously unexplored comparison, the main focus of this critique will be devoted to the ambivalent forces of hope and indeed hopelessness found inside Auschwitz concentration camp

---

17   Inside Time Prison Newspaper, August 2020, p.8, "Internment & IPP"

and what lessons we can learn from the survivors of the Holocaust.

In particular, one survivor provides us with an incredible insight into life inside Auschwitz - the psychotherapist, lecturer and writer, Victor Frankl. Born into a Jewish family in Vienna in 1905, Frankl soon became an influential member of a group of philosophers, mathematicians and scientists known as the Vienna Circle, which included Feud, Wittgenstein, Popper, Schoenbury, Carnap and Klimt. [18]

Fuelled by rampant anti-Semitism, the persecution of the Jews by the Nazis started with the boycott of Jewish businesses in 1933; the loss of citizenship in 1935 and the annexation of Austria in 1938. We learn Frankl first published texts on psychoanalysis in 1924 and went on to be one of *"the most important contributors in the field of psychotherapy since the days of Freud, Alder and Jung."*[19]

More specifically, Frankl gained recognition as a psychotherapist through the study of *"existentialism"*, which placed emphasis on *"the existence of the individual person as a free and responsible agent determining their own development through acts of the will".*[20]

This was quickly followed by Frankl's own psychotherapeutic theory of logo-therapy which stated the primary motivational force in man is to strive to find a meaning in one's life through the anticipation of beneficial opportunities in the future.

Sadly, four years later in 1942, Frankl's world came tumbling down when his entire family were seized and forcibly transported to Auschwitz concentration camp, where his parents, wife and brother were exterminated. Faced with a dire regime of slave

---

18   Malik, Kenan, The Observer, 24/05/20, p.16, Comment & Analysis
19   Frank, Viktor, (1959), "Man's Search for Meaning", p.155
20   Oxford English Dictionary, 11e Revised

labour, starvation and physical beatings, Frankl set his mind to create and develop a viable psychological hypothesis to counter the extreme psychopathological influences of the camp.

Of particular note, Frankl's keen observation of prisoners revealed *"there was sufficient proof that everything can be taken from a man but one thing: the last of the human freedoms – to choose one's attitude in any given circumstances, to choose one's own way"*.[21] In many respects, this observation chimes with IPP prisoners, who are wont to proclaim that the state may imprison one's physical body but not their free mind.

Frankl proclaimed there were always choices to make; the most prevalent being whether a prisoner was prepared to let the guards rob you of *"your very self, your inner freedom"*.[22] He claimed the sort of person a prisoner became was largely dependant upon his or her "inner decision". This process of survival was reinforced by the way the prisoners endured their suffering, which was interpreted as *"a genuine inner achievement"*.[23] He added, because *"suffering was an ineradicable part of life"*, it was no different to the vicissitudes of fate and even death. [24]

Frankl rationalized it was only those who maintained their *"inner strength"* and *"full inner liberty"* who could then go onto survive the horrendous influences of the camp, such as the physical beatings and exterminations.[25]

---

21   Frankl, Viktor, (1959), p.75
22   Ibid, p.75
23   Ibid, p.75
24   Ibid, p.76
25   Ibid, p.76

To some degree, the same applies to conventional long-term imprisonment in Britain. Firstly, whether correctly convicted or not, you are given a crushing indeterminate prison sentence and then forced to navigate your way through the most violent period in British penal history. For instance, in the year to March 2020, according to the Ministry of Justice, there were 22,210 prisoner-on-prisoner assaults; 9,784 assaults on staff and self-harm was up by 11% to 64, 552 reported incidents. Thankfully, self-inflicted deaths decreased by 13% from 87 to 76.[26]

Similar to serving IPP prisoners, Frankl stated:*"the most depressing influence of all was that a prisoner could not know how long his term of imprisonment would be".* [27] He added the prison term was not only *"uncertain"* but *"unlimited"* and was defined in terms of *"a provisional existence of unknown limit"*[28] which mirrors the sentence of an IPP prisoner. Analogous to concentration camp prisoners, over time IPP prisoners also allowed signs of deterioration and decay to set in and *"cease living for the future".*[29] Small wonder, out of the 194 deaths of IPP prisoners between 4 April 2005 and 31 December 2019, 63 were as a direct result of suicide. [30]

Frankl stated that a prisoner who frequently found himself in decline and believed that he had no future was usually preoccupied

---

26   Converse Prison Newspaper, August 2020, p.10, "Self Harm hi
        Record High"
27   Frankl, Viktor, (1959), p.78
28   Ibid, p.78
29   Ibid, p.79
30   FOIA response Ministry of Justice, No.200306016, dated 18/3/20

with *"retrospective thoughts"*. [31] The primary danger of looking to the past, made the horrors of the present *"less real"*.[32] More vitally, he claimed: *"in robbing the present of its reality there lay a certain danger"*, in the sense that it made prisoners overlook the positive opportunities of the camp *"which really did exist."*[33]

This may be observed in contemporary prison environments where over-tariff prisoners yield to taking drugs in order to numb reality, stop going to the gymnasium, spend more time in bed and generally withdraw from normal prison life. The maximum tariff of 999-months or 83.25 years is soul-destroying. Upon seeing these ghost-like figures, it is like someone has stuck a big syringe into their body and extracted all hope and purpose from their soul, and they give up.

Paradoxically, Frankl asserts, those who look back retrospectively at their life *"believed that the real opportunities in life had passed"* and that they had failed to view life in the camp as an opportunity , a challenge, an *"inner triumph"*. [34] In fact, Frankl's overriding mantra for those on the slide into mental and physical decay comes from Nietzsche, who proclaimed: *"He who has a why to live for can bear almost any how."*[35]

Frankl went further, when he said *"life ultimately means taking responsibility to find the right answer to its problems and to fulfil the task which it constantly sets for each individual".* [36] In as much

31   Frankl, Viktor, (1959), p.78
32   Ibid, p.80
33   Ibid, p.80
34   Ibid, p.81
35   Ibid, p.84
36   Ibid, p.85

as it does not matter what problems IPP prisoners face, there are right answers and it is up to them as individuals to seek them out and act upon them.

One of the key ways Frankl restored hope in those prisoners who were on the verge of losing their life was *"getting them to realise that life was still expecting something from them; something in the future was expected for them"*.[37] As he added: *"For no man knew what the future would bring, much less the next hour."*[38]

All in all, however, the crux of Frankl's philosophy (as narrated in his book *Man's Search for Meaning*) was that when prisoners in concentration camps, or indeed any other institutions, are feeling down and in *"existential vacuum, a feeling of emptiness or meaninglessness"*, then they should respond by looking to the future and seeking out their meaning and purpose in life.[39]

According to the concept of logotherapy, we can find the meaning of life in three specific ways. Firstly, by creating a work or doing a deed, such as learning a trade or writing and publishing a book. Secondly, by experiencing something or encountering someone new to love and respect. Thirdly, by the *"attitude"* we take toward unavoidable suffering, such as viewing suffering as an opportunity or challenge to acquire an inner triumph.[40]

Essentially, the author believes that what Frankl is trying to say - and does so with persuasive eloquence - is it does not matter how bad things get; even being in a concentration camp, surrounded

---

37   Ibid, p.87
38   Ibid, p.90
39   Ibid, p.143
40   Ibid, p.115

by suffering and death of unimaginable magnitude. The important thing is that we should confront fate with hope in our hearts and courage in our step.

Viktor Frankl passed away in 1997 aged 92. He sold 9 million copies of his book. What a man!

A Figment of My Emancipation

By S. T

Author's note: *"My story is about the horror of being in some terrible place, considering my place in the universe and my symbolic rebirth."*

Part 1: Solitude eternal

In the absence of light, obsequious retinae absorb the void. Cones seek out grey in the blackness and rods occasionally report red, deep red. Maybe that's just blood in my eyes. I do not know who I am, or what I am, or where I am. I have discordant memories. I recall pain; was it yesterday or was it years ago? Are there others like me? Maybe here in the blackness with me? I feel the echo of someone else. A nebulous recollection. It is an aching, a longing, a feeling that I was not always alone. Somewhere, in the deepest recesses,where hazy memories hide, I see glimpses of another life. Moonlight on a still lake, sunlight on my face, walking in the rain with... someone.

I remember now, I remember the blood, so much blood, then the dream, then the blackness. I remember I did not want the blackness (or red), I wanted nothing; quietus. Oh, what have I done? Perhaps this is just a transition to absolute nothingness. A lifetime in a fraction of a second before oblivion. It was not supposed to be like this.

There; a sound. Still my racing mind. I listen. Fear, like a straitjacket, subdues me.

There, something moved. My eyes are open, I focus. I see deep red walls, wet organic walls. Pulsing pillars of adipose, oozing vicious, putrescent waxes. Amorphous shapes throb at the edge of my vision. I am not alone. Angst, trepidation, terror. I am not alone. I see a figure before me; I advance toward it; it mirrors my every movement, mocking me. Who am I? I ask.

You are no one, you never were.

Where am I?

You are nowhere, you fool, you always will be.

Who are you?

Who am I? You really do not know? Like you, I once had a life. I breathed clean, sweet air. I saw light, such beautiful bright light. Like you, I watched my life blood spill from me. But it does not end there, does it?

The figure comes close to my face. A vision of suffering; it's breath as cold as death. I stumbled. Reaching out, I grabbed it's shoulders - and the mirror fell from my hands, smashing into a thousand pieces. Each shard, for a moment, reflecting blinding light and fragmented faces from deep within my memory. Weeping, wretched faces, mouths contorted in desperate cries. And then the blood red fades into black. I remembered everything. In the absence of light, I plucked out my eyes. I have no use for them now. I sat down, alone, in pitiful solitude and stared into the black, forever.

Part Two: Birth Pains

Mankind seem to enjoy suffering, creating abstract concepts such as sin, guilt, pity and fear. So he suffered, oh how he suffered. The pathetic blind man, in that dark, cold place, with just the phantoms of his contrition for company. For an aeon his suffering, his pain and his lassitude were immeasurable. And then the madness took him. The walls became warm and pulsed with a life force. The walls held him, cradled him, in loco parentis. In truth, he did not go mad - he could not. He had no mind, no consciousness; he just was.

Then, after an aeon, he found himself floating with an infinity of atoms in space. Now he had form; Quark, Proton, Neutron. For a billion years he was a sun; he was God. He gave life and sustained life and took life - without pity, without remorse. When he tired of being God, he became Supernova; he became spiral galaxies. He sucked all life from the universe, with a very big bang, and gave birth to a million suns. As stardust he formed a world. He composed a symphony of fire and ice, a cacophony of raging seas and crashing mountains. Then he bought calm. He was dust on the wind, a pebble on a riverbed, a leaf gently falling from a tree, a neuron forming in a foetus. It was then he felt the energy, the spark. He gave birth to a thought and that thought became flesh. He opened his eyes and when they calmed and focused, he began to make out a shape. He looked down at his hands; he was holding a knife. He dropped the blade. With the realisation of what he had done, he wept. A tear formed and fell. Within that tear was everything that had ever been and all that would come to pass. An infinite ocean; a sea of dreams.

Part Three – Tide Pools

Below the surface, the darkest depths hold unimaginable mysteries. Sinking, deeper and deeper, the blackness overwhelms and becomes one with the void. Tentacles of trans-dimensional beings materialise and disappear, leaving glowing trails, dancing and spiralling as they fade into the emptiness where multiverses collide. Ghostly humanoid figures watch silently, spectral sentinels at a gateway between worlds. Bioluminescent things swim. Some, benign lovers, embracing as they emerge into the great chasm. Some, all teeth and violent energy, seeking to devour all that illuminates the void. Overhead, high above, the light from a full moon penetrates the surface, calling him from the depths. The silver rays reach down, bestowing salvation and the purging of his sins, offering benediction. On the surface a storm rages. Waves of unimaginable magnitude rise, moonlight painting their Zenith white, then crashing into the oceanic chaos. Violent tempests whirl, dragging vast choirs into vortices.

He rushes toward the angry surface, laughing and screaming. A broken corpse and an unborn child. He breaks through into the wild air, gasping his first breaths. Flesh torn, eyes wide open, alive. The waves carry his body towards the shore, caressing him, healing his wounds, making him whole. The scales of karma balanced, the akashic records neatly filed.

The waves recede, leaving tide pools on the shore. Each pool a microcosm, a world within a world.

He awakens on a beach, lying naked, like a starfish. He opens his eyes, blinking in the sunlight.

He remembers nothing.

From Learner to Teacher

By Christopher A

Coming up to my twentieth year in prison, on a life sentence, I had an experience which taught me how fragile my belief in the future is. It was a momentary exchange between myself and an officer, a few words, which, when compared to the stress of meeting with officials, seems almost trivial. For example, I have now sat in front of five parole hearings and listened to senior officers who have been sent by the prison to describe me, my personality and my behaviour. Yet, not once have I known these officers beyond greeting them as we passed in the corridor.

Similarly, on two occasions I have sat and listened to psychologists hired to "assess" me. Both had spent a couple of hours discussing my life before writing reports which curiously agreed with those of the prison service which hired them. All their assessments also happened to contradict the in-depth reports of the psychologists who I have lived with for three years now at Brixton Prison's 'London Pathways Unit' (LPU). The first parole board psychologist wrote an analysis of my fictional works, without reading any of them. When challenged, she admitted that she had written what she had been told by the prison and that she had neither seen nor received any evidence to support it. The second told the parole panel that I had problems relating to my wife because she wanted forms of sex that I would not carry out.

Challenged to name them, she admitted it was untrue and that she had invented the accusation. Furthermore, she could not explain why such an invention was even relevant, when I was in prison for the murder of one white man by another during an argument over money. Despite this, she had spent over two hours discussing interracial sex, just because my wife is West Indian while I am 'White English.' Oddly, on both of these occasions, the chair of the parole panel refused to allow me time to investigate or reply.

Yet despite such events, my time on the LPU has left me hopeful. I had arrived after almost a decade of believing I would never be released and lacking any trust in either the uniformed prison staff or the plain-clothed probation and psychological staff. What changed this - what resurrected hope in my heart - was the chance to talk with staff members. In one-to-one sessions and group work I began to respond to them as human being, rather than bureaucrats. Within a month or two I had spoken more with staff than I had in a decade and a half at HMP Swaleside. I found my view of life lifting, as the phrase I used *"If i am ever released"* was constantly challenged with the phrase *"when you are released"*. Slowly the pipe dream that I would one day live with my wife again and have a career which gave my life value solidified and became a reasonable aspiration. For the first time in prison I felt that I was being treated not as a "lag", but rather as a human being.

And here I need to pause, because I'm giving a misleading impression. It is not that good and pleasant things haven't happened in prison - they have. But what these events failed to do was give me hope for the future. Pleasant though they were, they spoke only to the moment. For example, I am a strong Christian with a background in congregation-led worship. As you can imagine, a prison chapel - led by priests who see it as their duty to speak down to the lost and fallen - has not been wholly positive. Yet on two occasions Chaplains (both C of E) have reached out to those of us from different traditions. One allowed a prisoner-led service every six weeks. The other made space every week for inmates to speak. Of all the spiritual experiences in prison, it is these two which make me feel I still belong to the church.

Then there was the discovery of writing for pleasure. I came into prison after my fortieth birthday having always wanted to write. I had done amateur dramatics and been the person who pulled our improvisation into shape, but the idea of writing a play from beyond scratch was beyond me. Until, that is, I met Irene Garrow - our writer in residence. It was she who encouraged me to move on from the occasional poem. That led to the excitement of competitions: the Koestler, the Prison Reform Trust and Synergy. Just like Irene's workshops, the best thing was getting feedback - good or bad, it helped. On one occasion I tried a screenplay and people loathed it - too long and too complicated; they seemed to be struggling to find anything good to say about it. Except over and over again, people liked two minor characters, teenage girls added for a bit of light relief who spent the film bitching at each other. So, I pulled them out and rewrote their story for the radio. It won platinum (highest level) in Koestler.

Finally, I flaked into something I hope will be my life *"when"* I am released. I discovered the wonder of teaching. Many years ago, with a bad degree in an odd subject (Modern European Literature and Philosophy), I considered teaching. Trouble was, I didn't have the empathy to make a teacher. However, in prison I was between jobs and Education were short of classroom assistants, so when offered a temporary job I took it. Within a month, I knew this was what I was put on Earth to do. I discovered that patience can be learnt; that as you work with a student you begin to care about them. I worked with a tutor who saw my interest and taught me phonics. A teacher who recognised what I did well and built that into lesson plans; she would run the main class, whilst I would take students aside for one-to-one work on their weak points. Yet none of these good things encouraged me to look into the future. I had accepted life in prison as my future and worked to make it as pleasant as possible; not to be released.

It was only when I moved to the LPU that I, with the help of the staff, began the process of believing that one day I could be or "would be" free. However, as I said at the beginning of this piece - it is a very fragile state. Let me explain...

Recently I was asked to attend the lockdown activities committee. This meant I had to bang on my door to be opened up. When it was, I asked to be taken to the chapel where the meeting was to take place. The officer paused and asked: *"but how do I know the meeting is even happening?"* I swear I almost mistook myself for a person to be trusted, not a prisoner who could be easily assumed to be lying. I almost answered *"because I've just told you"*, but instead I remembered who I am and suggested she ring the chapel to check.

They tell me to say *"when I am released"*, but when would they release a man so untrustworthy he can't be trusted to tell the truth about a meeting on the prison noticeboard?

Hope, as Kafka once wrote, is there in infinite amounts for the decent of the world. But, for those like me, will it ever truly exist?

Seg

By J.J

I am a segregation expert. First three weeks for some bumped up charges with some 'misbehaviour' thrown on top, then a month – and now I was looking at a little longer in what they so pleasantly call 'close custody.' It isn't that hard, really. Once you know the power of detachment, of letting go, you discover a kind of freedom. Even when I was free, how much 'control' was there? How much do those lucky sods outside these many walls really have? They probably don't ask such a question – until it matters.

Trapped inside this shitpit, I've created entirely new worlds within the ephemeral realm of thought. They could be worlds of loss, based on memories of the past, or worlds of fantasy, based on anything at all. If you try hard enough, you can paint a novel from the patterns on a concrete wall. Mind over matter, thoughts over actions, memories over events. If you can sketch a hell like heaven and glimpse the light in darkness, seeing rainbows in the darkest storms, hope can be found. It is easy to write about, but hard to understand. And, while it is true that I can be content for many days with just paper and a pen, I can still experience immense frustration that sometimes erupts in fire. That's where the in-cell workouts can help a little.

Routine is everything. 30 minutes out of cell, pacing around a concrete yard. Three meals, or two if you discount the plastic packet of cereal and milk they call breakfast. Sometimes I try to spice it up a bit with the salt and pepper sachets that appear randomly for some dinners. Yeah, you'd be surprised how much a bit of seasoning can improve the taste of UHT milk.

Then it's onto some crusty old book published last decade, followed by a bit of writing. And sleeping. Lots of sleeping. You can probably guess which part I'm doing now... unless – well, I haven't even seen The Matrix so why pretend I'm living inside it?

They can fuck the TV. Last one they tried to push on me got smashed up. Still paying for it, actually.

In my first month of Seg, I quickly learned that the screws are a little different from the rest of the prison. They work in shifts, like everywhere, but the ones down here come in two extremes: would-be social workers and down-right nasty pieces of work. I seem to have a talent in attracting the latter ones. Whether it's keeping you waiting around for a toilet roll when you're desperate to go, or some snide comment trying to provoke, the best way to deal with it is ignoring them. That isn't always easy, however.

On the last 'cell inspection' I had the delight in greeting a gentleman I'll refer to as Mr Z. Probably best if I keep his description capped at that. He is a man – or looks like one – so that'll do.

Mr Z came striding in, straight to the small aperture they call a window with a metal mesh over it, and frowned.

"You've been trying to remove this?"

I stared at the immovable metal and shook my head.

"We'll have to do a full search in case."

So in come his two colleagues as I wait outside.

Bang. Laughter. More banging. Ten minutes pass.

They file out, and Mr Z is wearing a kind of lopsided grin that reminds me of a dog cartoon character from Dick Dastardly or something.

He was holding up a squashed and sodden toilet roll, somewhat misshaped into... yeah. Now I know where Dick Dastardly had come from.

"I guess you'll be needing this," he chuffed, flinging the sodden roll onto the bed.

I stared at it and back at his smirking colleagues. Then I laughed. "Oh, thanks Guv. Appreciate the gift."

Going by the force at which he subsequently shut my door, that response was probably a mistake. Should have just stayed silent.

*

The others here come and go. Across the hall was some youngster who looked barely out of his teens, apparently a self-harmer. Every hour they peeped into his cell, checking that he wasn't trying to slit his wrists or hang himself. I couldn't see how either was possible, given that he had nothing to do it with, but that's prison for you. Next to me used to be Yorkie – some beefed up Yorkshireman who loved getting into fights. He used to spend all his time of 'recreation' cleaning his cell. Thirty minutes, every day. Mopping, sweeping, spraying. That guy had an issue.

With Yorkie gone, I'm probably the longest resident now. I can't tell if they're pissed at having me so long, or if they take some perverse delight in trying to annoy me. Pushing the buttons, as if I'm one of those PlayStation consoles from the 90s. Couldn't they have got a job driving a forklift, or even just staying at home drinking beer and pretending to be Lara Croft...?

No matter. They're with me, and I'm with them. We might as well play this little game to the end.

Three years. Tick tock, tick tock. This is some shitty game. And yet it's not a game, is it? No mate, it's my life. And others lives – those I stole from, and the family I still have outside. If ever there was a game, I lost it badly long ago.

Let's not bother rehearsing the pathways that might have been, the turnings that were never taken. That's taken up most of my sentence already. Even now, in the background of dildo-making screws and crazed Yorkshiremen, there is meant to be some kind of appeal with me and my co-defendants. It could make the difference between three more years and... none.

To think, if it goes well, I could be leaving these walls! When I dwell on the outside world, it is easier for me to remember how it smelled. The fresh scent of crushed autumn leaves; the revved-up fumes of petrol; my partner's apricot perfume. My cousin, who spent 5 years inside, used to always say that smell is more intense when you leave jail. Messed up drug addict, but I have a feeling our noses aren't too different.

Whether I'll keep smelling this musty, sweaty shitpit or something much nicer for years depends on three wigged-up old men sitting in London's Court of Appeal.

Another day passes, another night. I sit hunched up against

the wall, pouring through the lawyer's casework. A pain builds up behind my eyes as the hours inch closer to morning.

There is a knocking at the door.

A face frames the small aperture. It is Miss James.

For a moment my mind plays a trick, telling me she is some entity sent from heaven.

"Are you okay, John?"

She is the first guard to call me by my first name.

I paused, not knowing what to say.

Who are you…? Part of me wondered.

"Yes, I'm fine thanks, just going through some legal paperwork."

She smiled. "Okay, don't stay up too late!"

I blinked as the window shutter closed.

*

Haven't seen Miss James for a month now. I hope she'll be back soon.

Find the Flocking Hope

By Martin F

There are times in life when traumatic experiences are vacuum-packed into your mind's eye. The whole incident replayed again and again as it happens, whilst your heartbeat holidays and you are frozen to the spot by some sort of magical spell cast by the white witch.

The enemy of hope is despair, and despair's closest associate is helplessness; they reside in the lair of the misfortune cartel. We have all felt helpless from time to time, but my most recent episode was in my neighbour's prison cell. I stopped across the threshold to watch him plummet from the roof area with all the ungainly slapstick a clown if he were to nose-dive from the circus high tower into a paddling pool of custard.

Thud.

Unfazed but a little unsteady, I helped him to some food whilst all the wing's witnesses cho:

'*What are you doing, Herbert?*"

Herbert is a budgie. Not just any budgie, a prison budgie. He stands a feisty four inches tall and is the blue and white of the old prison button shirts. He only knows prison and was born in an establishment within the high-security estate. His flock are people - mostly murderers, robbers and arsonists, and he loves them all. As a tiny fledging only a few weeks old, he was rejected by his mother but rescued by his current cellmate who had to spend hours and hours feeding him and building up his strength. He was never denied access to other budgies, but is so imprinted on humans that he thinks he is one and is uninterested in other birds. He can whistle, talk and is even capable of 'persuading' you out of any edible goodies you may have purchased from the prison canteen. He's even so brave he will nibble at prison food, fully accepting of the inevitable resulting upset tummy.

I have known Herbert years - he even lived on the last wing I was on in my former prison. So tame, he would fly and glide where he wanted. Acrobatically he would sidestep people, and occasionally crop dust the odd tattooed neck or bald scalp. He would land on the shoulder of the ping-pong player, then perch on the edge of the snooker table for a squawk at the shiny cue ball. When finally bored he would high-speed aim for his cell and bark like a dogfighting spitfire through the door!

Once in a while, the misfortune cartel conspires with circumstance to disadvantage their victim. One fateful evening an unpleasant blistering heat overtook the prison's landings, accelerating Herbert's feather moult. The morning revealed a floor full of feathers, more akin to an accident in a Brobdingnag duvet factory than the usual OCD cleanliness we were all used to.

Herbert could not fly!

His innate power, his mobility, his freedom, robbed by prematurely discarded flight feathers. Loud upset gasps resonated along the prison corridors as Herbert's flock learnt of his fate, and the vain futile panicky wing flaps could be persistently heard for a few weeks after. The universe in support sent all positive charged atmospheric ions to its segregation block, thus in empathy enabling a period of mourning. The light days felt darker, unpleasant smells more pungent, and the usual sounds of prison were uglier.

As time passed, new flight feathers emerged, but the jester of circumstance sent them off-kilter. The beauty of the appearing light-blue down was no substitute for feathers. Herbert's flightlessness looked long-term.

Adaptability is key to prison survival, and Herbert quickly learnt to play with the hand he was dealt. Perches were strategically erected to enable sensible hops and increase his independent cell streaks. When necessary he learnt to let out a deafening shriek, like some sort of mafioso godfather commanding his flock lieutenants to support his movements. From shoulder to index finger, from head to wrist, he would bounce where necessary in order to arrive at any desired destination. He seemed to have overcome his flightlessness; he had discovered his new way.

During this tumultuous time, as during all times, men would appear and 'level up' on animal therapy. Life sentences create unknown futures for people; flaccid goals and tender anxieties. Non-judgemental platonic love is often void in penal institutions, but Herbert selflessly plugs that gap.

Forlorn human-beings trapped by systems and circumstances can lose hope. However, the loss of hope is a choice; we are in charge of this power. The vile misfortune cartel may employ illusionary devices to snatch it from the quiver of survival, but your own personal hope can only be accessed by negative forces if you allow yourself to lose resolve. Protection of this may sound simple, but years of imprisonment have shown tough individuals crippled when ill-prepared neurotic defences of their hopes and dreams are invaded by the Misfortune Cartel's attack squads.

Even during the eternal support given to all men deep in their own personal psychological wars, Herbert remained resolute. Flight is intrinsic to the definition of a budgie; an evolutionary earned status in the animal kingdom. To lose the ability must feel like an assault on identity, on motivation, on purpose. Yet never have I seen Herbert's beak drop lower than his perch. His head remains proud. Never will he surrender his hope, defending it with all the pride of Duma's Musketeers.

Life's most mighty lessons always seem amplified when their challenges previously appeared unendurable. They provide inspiration, creating arrows for hope's quiver. Herbert the budgie, in his four inches, is inspirational.

On occasions he will attempt a perch launch – but, alas, none of his pitch attempts are yet to be successful. However, my oxymoronically flightless budgie neighbour never gives up. He is always armed with an arrow of hope! He still loves his flock, and if he were ever to meet you would instantly adopt you without initiation. Any special 'love parcels' that fall from his derriere would be accidental, not an ornithological version of fraternity hazing.

Despite the elusive power of flight being absent, the positive atmospheric ions are back and fully charged. The days are brighter, smell sweeter, and prison noises more musical. Herbert's misfortune cartel has been contained. He did it, and when presented with any adversity so can we all.

So, follow Herbert's lead. Keep your beak above your perch, embrace life and when necessary shield your hope! Never surrender it.

Herbert does, and one day he will fly again.

About the Arkbound Foundation

The Arkbound Foundation, a small charity setup in 2017, aims to support people from diverse and marginalised backgrounds through the powers of writing. Aside from publishing books by these people, with a priority for ones that cover important social or environmental themes, we also provide mentoring placements so that aspiring writers can develop their skills with an experienced author or literary agent.

Writing Within Walls is part of a project of the same name, setup to provide opportunities for people in custody and those who have been newly released from custody. The twenty pieces in this book represent the winning entries of a national writing competition that we conducted in 2020.

If you would like to find out more, please visit **www.arkfound.org** or write to: Arkbound Foundation, Backfields House, Upper York Street, Bristol BS2 8QJ.

BV - #0029 - 140521 - C0 - 203/127/8 - PB - 9781912092161 - Matt Lamination